AIR BRIDGE 1

The story of the civilian vehicle air ferry
from 1947 to 1963

Paul A Doyle

and

David M Pugh

Forward Airfield Research Publishing >

First published in 2006 by
Forward Airfield Research Publishing
14 Clydesdale Road
Royston, Hertfordshire   SG8 9JA

ISBN 0 9525624 2 1

Typesetting by the Doyles

Printed and bound in England by
Woolnough Bookbinding Ltd.
Express Works, Church Street
Irthlingborough, Northants NN9 5SE

By the same author/publisher:

Fields of the First - A history of aircraft landing grounds in Essex
used during the First World War
Where the Lysanders were ... (the story of Sawbridgeworth's airfields)
Air Bridge 2 - The design, development and service use of the ATL98 *Carvair*
conversions and their effect on the civilian vehicle air ferry era
Aviation Memorials of Essex - a gazetteer of the memorials to feats of aviation
in the County, and the story behind each

Front cover photograph:

A scene evocative of vehicle air ferry activities, passengers for Freighter Mk 31E G-AMLP
'Vanguard' of Air Charter are escorted to the aircraft at Southend by the steward whilst their
vehicles are being loaded. Unlike many sequences taken of these operations, this was not a
'posed' shot, as is evident by the casual flight line worker on the fuselage and the propellors
not set to 'parade-ground' squareness (photo by Richardsons, Leigh on Sea, Essex). See also
penultimate picture in book showing the aircraft after conversion to Mk 32 standard.

Contents

Acknowledgements   iv
Photographic credits   iv
Introduction   v

Chapters:

From little acorns.....   1
The early days   1

Silver City Airways 1948-53   4
The building of Lydd Airport   24
Silver City Airways 1954 (the end of Lympne)   34
Silver City Airways 1954-59   35
Murmerings of a new vehicle-ferry aircraft....   69
Silver City Airways 1959 (contd)-62   70

Aviation Traders Ltd   84
The Accountant Saga   86
Fairflight Ltd   89
Surrey Flying Services Ltd   89
Air Charter Ltd   90
The Channel Air Bridge 1954-1963   91

Conclusions   100
Comparison in cross-Channel routing, 1962 & 1971   101

Appendices:

1 Conversion tables   102
2 Data for Bristol Freighter aircraft   102
3 G/As of Bristol 170 Freighter Mk 31 & Superfreighter Mk 32   103
4 Silver City Airways vehicle ferry services from 1948-54   104
5 Silver City Airways example timetable for 1953 summer season   105
6 Silver City statistics from 1948-54   105
7 Silver City Airways vehicle ferry services from 1955-62   106
8 Silver City statistics from 1955-62   109
9 Histories of aircraft used by Silver City Airways   110
10 Histories of aircraft used by Air Charter Ltd   114

Bibliography   120
Author's pages   120

Acknowledgements

Between 1974-77 many people, primarily ex-vehicle ferry operatives, were interviewed about the cross-channel vehicle ferry era, every contact thus made resulted in us being welcomed into their homes or offices, which in so doing took up much of their valuable time. To all those who helped in our researches, especially those persons still in the aircraft industry at the time we dealt with them, either by memory-jogging or the supply of information and photographs so that this story could be told, our grateful thanks are extended.

Principal thanks are due to my colleague, David Pugh, who contributed most to the text of this book. The results of his researches, the most detailed ever produced and relating to the embryonic days of the vehicle air ferry, were realised over the course of many hours during 1974-79, and form the bulk of this work.

Since 2000, when *Air Bridge 2* was published, pressing family problems dictated that work on this volume be paused temporarily, followed by a period of contacting people again for their reminiscences. To those people who enjoyed *Air Bridge 2*, and were disappointed that this work was late in arriving, I can only apologise and trust that the wait was worth it.

Grateful thanks to:

John Allan, Consultant Aeronautical Design Engineer, Bembridge
Ken Bailey, Maintenance Engineer, Lydd Airport (Silver City Airways)
Len Birch, Maintenance Engineer, Lydd Airport (SCA)
Cliff Bishop, Design Liason Engineer, Stansted (Aviation Traders Engineering Ltd)
Dr R N E Blake, Senior Lecturer in Town Planning, Nottingham Trent University
British Rail Shipping & International Services Division
Ken Cole (British Air Ferries), Southend
Keith Dagwell (Chairman, Silver City Association), East Sussex
Department of Transport, Australia
Department of Transport and Power, Eire
the late Mike B de Woolfson, Commandant, Lydd Airport (SCA)
Janice and Christopher Doyle
Anthony English, Captain (SCA), Norfolk
Freddie Foster (SCA & BAF), Southend
the French Embassy, London
Tim Hall (*Aeroplane* magazine), London
Norris Heritage, (SCA/Hurds), Lydd Airport
Harry Holmes, Manchester
Ken Honey, Cornwall
Dave Hutchinson, Captain (SCA/BUAF), Norfolk
Maurice Jeffrey (BAF)
Sebastian Pooley (Pooleys Flight Guides), Elstree
National Ports Council, London
Paul Purser, Leigh on Sea
Jack Robins, Captain (SCA)
Gerry Rosser, Captain (SCA)
Mike Rossi, Traffic Superintendant (SCA & BUAF), Lympne/Lydd
John Taylor, Bembridge Airport
Secrétariat D'etat Aux Transports, France

Photographs

Unless credited otherwise, photographs are from the Silver City Airways collection amassed by David M Pugh during the course of collating this work in 1977.

Introduction

In 1974, just as the UK vehicle air ferry was coming to an end with the drawdown from service of the ATL98 *Carvair*, a colleague and I toyed with the idea of writing a history of the type. Over the course of three years we toured both this country and the channel coast of Europe to meet people who had been concerned with the cross-Channel vehicle air ferry, and corresponded with overseas operators, and after a short while were of the opinion that the air ferry concept proper had started after the end of the Second World War with the resurgence of the various private airlines which sprang up.

When research started the intention was to relate the day-to-day workings of the vehicle air ferry with British and French operators on the short-haul, cross-Channel routes from 1960, however it was found necessary to dig deeper and record not only the history of all the aircraft designs considered and the actual types used from the time of the 're-birth' of civil airlines after the dark days of the Second World War, but the historical origins of the companies operating them both before and during the period under consideration.

This volume focusses on the service use of the Bristol Freighter vehicle ferry types, and gives an outline of the working practices employed by the companies using this venerable workhorse from 1946 to 1963(-ish). Also included are the other aircraft types considered for use, or 'inherited' by company takeovers or amalgamation. For the period from 1962-1977 the reader should refer to the companion volume *Air Bridge 2*, which deals with the Aviation Traders ATL98 *Carvair* as a logical replacement for the Bristol Freighter.

Paul A Doyle
Royston, Herts 2005

For my parents,
and to all the people who put the 'buzz' into the vehicle air ferry trade

In between cars and passengers the air ferries were frequently involved with the carriage of horses and livestock. Here a mother and foal are about to be led into a Freighter Mk 32 at Hurn (photo by Photec, Woking, Surrey)

The car ferry wasn't around when these cars were built, but it seems a good way to start off. Veteran cars being loaded into Bristol Freighter Mk 32 G-ANVR 'Valiant' of Channel Air Bridge at Southend on 15 May 1958 for the 3rd International Rally of Automobile Ancestors at the Brussels World Exhibition. On the ramp is a 1912 De Dion Bouton drophead coupe, behind that a 1900 Orleans, then a 1913 Unic, and in front a 1900 Phebus Aster 2-seater (vehicle verification by the Veteran Car Club, Ashwell, Hertfordshire).

From little acorns.....

In 'The Aeroplane' of 13 June 1947 the correspondent of the Air Transport Affairs Section wrote:- "I saw somewhere the other day that it costs £8-10s-0d to ship a car across to France by sea, and that all the shipping space for this purpose is now booked up for July and August. Which charter company will be first to establish a regular car ferry across the Channel, using a Bristol Freighter and an Aerovan?

There is a gap of but 25 miles to be bridged for car owners between Dover and Calais and assuming that a two-way traffic was organised it should be perfectly feasible to compete with the Southern Railway. On ordinary single charters over longer distances the normal charge per mile for a Freighter is 10/- and for the Aerovan about 3/-, and at these rates the 25-mile trip would cost only £12-10-0 and £3-15-0 respectively for the two aircraft.

The Freighter will carry two ten-horsepower cars or one very large car, and the Aerovan one ten-horsepower car. Assuming that, with the establishment of a regular ferry service, these rates could be lowered considerably, on the face of it an air Channel car ferry should become a regular all-the-year-round institution. On that basis it would be worth turning a large field at Dover and one at Calais into Customs aerodromes.

Such an arrangement need not be a 'regular service' within the meaning of the Act, because each flight could be booked as a separate charter by the car owner"

The above article may or may not have been the very first comment on the vehicle air ferry concept, but those projected thoughts did gain a response. The first was from a correspondent who thought that the vehicle ferry idea was not a viable proposition because of the unsuitability of the Freighter, the second was a report that, at the beginning of July 1947, a Mr and Mrs Adams were to hire an Aerovan of Air Contractors Ltd to fly them with their car from Croydon to Le Touquet at the start of their honeymoon. This report concluded with the statement that, subject to Air Contractors having secured a return load, the one-way trip for car and occupants was to cost around £15-0-0.

However incredible it may seem now, these seemingly irrelevant happenings were to prove an extremely accurate prediction of future events. By coincidence, Mr and Mrs Adams were to re-appear on 24 February 1959, when they took part in an interview on the British Broadcasting Corporation's programme 'Mainly for Women', the subject under discussion being 'the ease of taking cars on holiday'.

The Early Days

It was not until June 1948 that there was any suggestion of the charter company Silver City Airways having in mind a project to transport vehicles by air to the Continent. This was made through the good offices of the Automobile Association and Royal Automobile Club, whose brochures offered to carry a car and four passengers from Lympne Airport in Kent to Le Touquet in France in 20 minutes for a one-way all-in fare of £32.

The birth of the idea owed much to the imagination and enthusiasm of Silver City Airways' managing director, Air Commodore Griffith James Powell CBE, RAF (retd) who, it is said, had been inspired in the possibilities of such a venture after Mr Leslie McCracken (who became the company's traffic manager when they moved headquarters to Great Cumberland Place) had suggested it would be good if one could drive cars into the front of a Freighter.

Born in Cardiff on 11 August 1907, Air Commodore 'Taffy' Powell left Bristol University in 1926 to take up a service commission in the RAF but resigned after four years to join Imperial Airways, where he piloted various services between Europe, the Middle East and South Africa. In 1936 he became the first Briton to gain a Masters certificate in both landplanes and flying boats, whilst the following year saw him very heavily involved in pioneering trans-Atlantic flights using modified 'Empire' class flying boats, as well as piloting the first Short 'Cambria' flying boat across the North Atlantic.

He was then appointed managing director of Imperial Airways (Bermuda) Ltd, which had its headquarters in New York, and given responsibility for the American side of the flying boat operation. With the outbreak of the Second World War he joined the RAF in Canada, and soon after the establishment of the Atlantic ferrying system joined the new RAF Ferry Command where he became Senior Air Staff Officer to Air Marshel Sir Frederick Bowhill, and subsequently became SASO of No 45 Group, RAF, with its widespread transport commitments. In 1943 he was awarded the CBE for this work, and on return to civil life became involved in the formation of British Aviation Services Limited.

Registered on 27 November 1945 British Aviation Services Ltd was formed with a nominal capital of £50,000, as a subsidiary of the British Aviation Insurance Company, its principal purpose being to serve as their technical branch. It was described as 'able to provide expert advice, trained personnel, and guidance or assistance in connection with the construction, operation, maintenance and repair of aircraft'. In relation to the development of aviation they were to 'carry on the business of manufacturers and operation of, and dealers in, aircraft and accessories, insurance brokers and agents etc, with the exception of airline operation'.

The directors at the time of the companys' formation were:-
Mr Edward B Ferguson, general manager of the Phoenix Assurance Company (chairman),
Mr Arthur S Rogers, general manager of the London & Lancashire Insurance Company,
Mr James D Simpson, chief general manager of Manchester Royal Insurance Company,
Captain A G Lamplugh, principal surveyor and underwriter of B.A.I.C, and
Air Commodore Griffith J Powell (managing director).

Operating originally from their headquarters at White Waltham the company moved out to Blackbushe when a contract to fly Dakotas out to Java was received in April 1946, indeed the company's services were well tailored for the growing aviation industry in the British Dominions, and it was in this capacity that the company carried out some of the most remarkable aircraft ferrying operations ever undertaken in modern civil aviation. This was achieved by supplying experienced pilots, of which around 60 had been drafted by Powell, to ferry surplus military and civil aircraft to numerous civil operators, of whom many had lost a large part of their fleet in the previous hostilities. Thus it was during the company's involvement in these foreign contracts that they were to become involved in the formation of Silver City Airways.

In 1946, with a general shortage of serviceable aircraft, the regular airline companies of the world were finding it difficult to operate normal pre-war schedules at a time when there was a demand for mining executives and engineering men to be flown between key points of the Commonwealth. In order to transport their mining men and machinery from Great Britain, South Africa, India, Malaya and Australia, the English and Australian mining interests in Broken Hill, New South Wales, who also had offices in London, sought advice from B.A.S. on the formation of their own airline. The company was subsequently formed with a nominal capital of £500,000 and registered in London on 25 November 1946 as Silver City Airways Limited, its name arose from the fact that the town of Broken Hill was known as the 'Silver City' of New South Wales, so called due to the rich silver deposits once found there.

The directors at the time of Silver Citys' formation were:-
Mr J V Govett, chairman of the Imperial Smelter Corporation,
Mr W S Robinson, joint managing director of the Zinc Corporation, and
Air Commodore Griffith J Powell, managing director of B.A.S.

The business of the company was also to operate between the United Kingdom and Australia with the aim of sponsoring companies, together with supplementary charter work, and to function in this capacity B.A.S's second Airspeed Consul that had been registered in their ownership at the beginning of July was supplemented by three Avro 691 Lancaster bombers. Converted to carry 19 passengers and renamed Lancastrians, they were also registered with B.A.S who were further implicated in the managing of the new company's interests through the directorship of Air Commodore Powell. The company subsequently operated another loaned Consul as well as purchasing one de Havilland Dove, two Douglas Dakotas and the prototype Lockheed 18-H Lodestar.

All three Lancastrians had made inaugural flights in Silver City livery by the beginning of December 1946 with the second, named 'City of Canberra', being the first aircraft to actually operate into Australia. Even at this time, long after the end of the Second World War, it was realised that a need still existed to fly VIPs about, so Powell had one of his Dakotas fitted out specifically as a VIP transport.

On the passenger side, Sir Winston Churchill was a regular traveller amongst the many military and political notables, this possibly having something to do with the fact that the Commodore had been for some time responsible for his travel arrangements during the Second World War. When the need for the private carriage of mining men and VIPs ceased with the re-establishment of the passenger airline schedules B.A.S, through its newly-formed trading subsidiary Britavia Limited (registered in May 1947), saw fit to accept all the Australian interests in Silver City Airways as part payment for their services. This therefore released the aircraft from any Australian commitment and also made the airlines' name available for B.A.S's sole use.

It is worth mentioning here that it was Britavia Limited who, in July 1949, announced an increase in share capital of £190,000 beyond its registered capital of £10,000. Of this B.A.S had, in December 1948, held 998 of the 1000 issued shares. The increase in capital therefore resulted in Britavia Limited becoming the holding company of Silver City and B.A.S's associated companies in Canada, Rhodesia and Malta (namely Britavia (Canada) Ltd, Northern Rhodesia Aviation Services Ltd and Air Malta Ltd), an arrangement undertaken to cater for the group's expansion. As a result of this reorganisation B.A.I.C disposed of its interests in B.A.S but retained the technical side of the operation which carried on under a new name.

Returning to Silver City Airways, the situation arose where they were forced to exist solely on charter work, and it was soon appreciated that the Lancastrians were unsuited to the normal cargo work generally required by most agents. Two of the aircraft, and one of the Dakotas, were therefore sold but the third Lancastrian, which had been registered in Silver City's ownership in September 1947, was retained until May 1948.

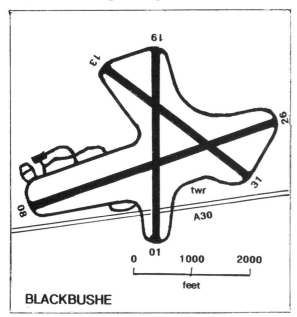

BLACKBUSHE

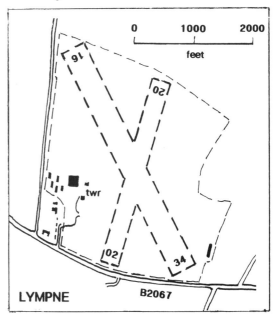

LYMPNE

(the airfield layouts show each site as it was during the relative period covered in the text)

Following this decision, and with the emphasis changing more to the carriage of freight, it was decided to to replace the sold aircraft by a single Bristol Type 170, so a 'solid' nosed Mk 2a 'Wayfarer' was obtained on loan from the Bristol Aeroplane Company. At this time 'loan' was the right way to go, as the cost of a new Freighter was in the order of £33,000 (the basic Wayfarer at this time was around £47,000, albeit a faster aircraft). The loaned aeroplane had been delivered to Suidair in April 1947 as ZS-BOM, but on return to Filton for repair after an engine failure at Rome during its first trip to South Africa, followed by a heavy landing at Croydon, it carried the name 'Silver City'. With Silver City as G-AHJG it carried out a number of limited charters and VIP passenger work until it was engaged on the Partition of India operation which had started in November 1947. For this it was based at Palam airport near Delhi and, minus seats, was used to transport Hindus out of Pakistan, pilgrims to Lahore, and Muslims out of India, and on one flight was reported to have had no fewer than 117 refugees on board.

Silver City Airways – 1948

However, by the spring of 1948 Silver City's Indian operations had reached an all-time low and 'HJG, which had been joined by a second Wayfarer 'HJC, were returned to Filton. The company then made arrangements for a Mk 1 Freighter, G-AGVC, to be fitted with nose loading freight doors in preparation for the proposed UK vehicle ferry charters.

G-AGVC, the first fully-equipped Freighter, had been on an extensive tour of North and South America where it flew 41,000 miles in 331 hours before being chartered to the Canadian Pacific Air Lines company for meat haulage around Venezuela. Conveniently it was returned to Filton in March 1948 and on 3 July, with the formalities of the new services provisionally completed, it was collected by Silver City's Captain 'Storm' Clark and First Officer P E 'Jerry' Rosser and delivered to Blackbushe. On 6 July it was then positioned to Lympne as the staging point for its first proving flight to Le Touquet that day, when it carried Air Commodore Powell's 16 hp Armstrong-Siddeley Lanchester, HXN 88. It then continued on to Le Bourget Airport, Paris where it stayed overnight.

When the Freighter returned to Le Touquet on 7 July the company quite unexpectedly had its first fee-earning cross-channel vehicle ferry charter from one Sammy Norman, who saw the aircraft land just as he was contemplating how to return to England as quickly as possible. His dilemma, or so they were told, was that he was unable to decide whether to do so with his Bentley or in his private aircraft, but after seeing Air Commodore Powell's car being secured within the hold of the Freighter he decided to part with 30,000 Francs to do likewise. The company assured him that this payment, the equivalent of £35, would ensure that he and his car would be flown to Lympne.

Although this was not the first vehicle to be air transported across the English Channel it was a very encouraging start and indicated that, under certain circumstances, a demand could indeed exist. Perhaps the most pleasing result of the exercise, at least as far as the company was concerned, was that it was witnessed by an insurance man who had flown over to Le Touquet in a light aircraft to observe, for insurance purposes, the method by which vehicles were carried.

Another six days passed then, on Tuesday 13 July, with the object of showing a press representation how much time their new charter service could save the prospective cross Channel travellor, Victor Charlie was once again eased up on a demonstration flight to Le Touquet. Carrying just 100 gallons of fuel which was the minimum, it was said, to allow for any emergency, the Freighter was brought to a standstill in France after a flight time of 17 minutes and a total block time of just under 25 minutes. On return to Lympne the service was continued on the basis of an average of one return flight per day.

When the Le Touquet service was inaugurated by Silver City a 'partner' company was also formed to assist in the French side of the operation. This company, Societé Commerciale

Aerienne du Littoral, was financed by Silver City and although initially non-operational very cleverly had the same initials (SCAL). Operated by the Le Touquet Airport Authority under Monsieur J H Sainsard it was also registered to give Silver City a legitimate claim against any prospective French company wishing to start a rival vehicle ferry service.

Needless to say during these early days the company's facilities were very primitive, indeed at Lympne the functions of receptionist, telephonist, traffic officer and car loader were all united in the priceless personage of Mr R G McRae. Until the start of the service Bob had been chauffeur to Mr W G Franklin – then the general managing director – and whilst his office consisted of a van the telephone belonged to the Ministry of Civil Aviation police who had first claim on it for their own recondite purposes. The only other staff consisted of two air crew, Captain Storm Clark and First Officer P E 'Jerry' Rosser, and two ground engineers. Customs examination and clearance of cars was conducted in a corner of the field, open to the elements but fenced round to deter sheep.

With regard to the Le Touquet side, the company representative there was a Kate Whelan who, whilst working alongside the new associate company (and provided with similar office accommodation to that at Lympne), was not quite expected to dash onto the aircraft to unload cars as this job was invariably done by the aircrew themselves.

However, whilst in this first term of serious operation the company was well satisfied with a total of 170 cars ferried up to the end of the experiment (and possibly including the four completed by Powell's own car on the proving flights), these early flights were not without their brief moments of humour. Possibly the most amusing of these concerned a party in Maidenhead one night where a certain gentleman, after having consumed a fair quantity of alcohol, bet a friend £100 that he and his car could be in Le Touquet by sun-up the next morning. The friend, being totally unaware of Silver City's air ferry due to it having been little-publicised by the media of the time, duly accepted the wager and later on that same evening the telephone at Lympne rang with a gentleman requesting that an aircraft be made ready half-hour before sun-up to fly him and his car to France.

The crew slept on the airfield to be ready at such an hour, the gentleman then duly turned up to be loaded along with his car and, on arrival at Le Touquet, asked the crew to await his return whilst he drove to the nearest telephone box which happened to be at the other side of the airfield. On his return, and to the astonishment of the crew, he promptly asked to be flown straight back to Lympne whereupon he finally declared the reasoning by which he had made a neat profit of £36, less his incidental expenses from Maidenhead.

It says much for the cross Channel air ferry that in the end, with this and many exploits by seemingly half-crazed Englishmen, one would not be surprised if mention of the air ferry was found in most textbooks on postwar industrial revolution. In fact, articles such as E S Turners 'The Channel Hop', published in 'Punch' of 2 April 1958, should be read if only to put the whole era into perspective.

With the establishment of the experimental vehicle ferry service the autumn of 1948 saw a period of unexpected activity for Silver City when Russian actions in Berlin led to what became known as the Berlin Airlift. During the middle of September the company's first Freighter, 'Victor Charlie', was soon employed on this operation after British European Airways, who had overall control of the airlift, had requested that additional aircraft be made available to fly supplies into Berlin and manufactured goods out. The initial aircraft at Hamburg was joined on 12 October by a second Freighter, G-AHJO (at the time registered to Bowater Limited) and then by three others, G-AGVB, 'HJC and 'IME, which had also been taken on loan from the Bristol Aeroplane Company. Although the experience gained on this charter during the winter of 1948 was to stand the company in very good stead in the years ahead, and despite them having been refused permission to operate the Freighters at a AUW of 42,000 lbs (i.e. an increase of 2,000 lbs), the aircraft were still too slow by comparison with the Douglas C54s and tended to throw the operation out of step, so for this reason the Freighters were eventually taken off the operation.

5

Back in England, and with his Freighters fully occupied with freight work left by the other charter companies still operating in Berlin, Powell soon appreciated that his aircraft would eventually be open to fierce competition when other companies returned from the Airlift. Therefore with the success of the 12-week air ferry operation which had officially ended on 7 October 1948 (but actually on the 4th) the company set about carrying out a larger scale experiment. In order to put this new service onto a firmer footing they then applied for a further licence to run the service, but this time on a scheduled basis.

Silver City Airways – 1949

In 1949, contrary to what might be believed, the procedure for one obtaining a licence to operate an international service was a complex one, and its granting automatically conferred reciprocal rights on the other nation. In addition to this it was then, and still applies now, always possible for a competitor to successfully veto the application. So it was, that the re-introduction of the 1949 ferry service was inaugurated on 13 April, but only after the company had successfully applied for a one year associate agreement licence with BEA and further reinforced the connection with their French counterpart. By this action the French company became for the first time fully air-operational with a single Freighter, later adding a second in 1950.

By the time that operations on the new service had started the combined staff at each airport had been increased to two car drivers and two traffic officers. A total of eight pilots were then employed, six English (Captains Rosser, C I Hopkins, D Flett, L A Madelaine, J Norton and M Davison) and two French, the first being a Captain Geraine, but the French pilots were not allowed to fly the British-registered Freighters and vice versa. Two English and two French flight engineers were also taken on but no radio operators were employed due to the aircraft carrying VHF radios operated from the pilots positions.

To Silver City's surprise the service soon exceeded all expectations. By the middle of June the 800th car had been carried, on 5 August the 1000th and on 11 November the 2500th, the busiest day being 28 July when 21 round trips by four Mk 170s carried a total of 63 cars. A monthly breakdown of the number of cars carried was as follows: April (from the 13th) 53, May 75, June 131, July 634, August 802, September 589, October 168 and November (to the 13th) 48. The total number carried for the year was 2600, whilst during the seven-month period between 13 April and 13 November the Mk 170s of Silver City and its French counterpart flew 90,000 miles and 1900 stage flights.

The growth of the operation during 1949 can also be shown by the regularity of services – its feasibility having been adequately demonstrated when the cheapest car on the British market was driven from London to Paris via the car ferry and beat the 'Golden Arrow' by one hour twenty minutes. In April and May the daily average was three to four flights, in June six, by early July twelve and from 28 July to the end of August sixteen round trips, although this frequency gradually tailed off towards the end of October. At this time it was decided to continue the service throughout the coming winter period, but with the running being limited to an 'on-demand' operation from 30 October. The service then continued in numerous irregularities until the normal scheduled service was resumed on 1 April 1950.

This winter service was not without incident though. In November, due to extremely bad flooding at Le Touquet, Freighter G-AGVB sank into the grass to the underside of its fuselage and was there for three days until it could be moved. The slight damage was soon rectified, and it was returned to service soon after being released.

As the 1949 season progressed, the air ferry traffic was found to be predominantly in one direction, outward from Lympne and homeward in September and October, and consisted of approximately 90% British and 10% French and American cars. This one-way trend however, when the aircraft were flying empty of vehicles in one direction, did allow bulk consignments of freight to be flown between the two airports at very attractive rates.

An example of this trade was when Air Affretment, a French forwarding and shipping agency, chartered a number of Silver City Bristol 170s during July to ship a total of 66 tons of fruit from Le Touquet to Lympne in 19 flights. In another instance a consignment of furnace refractory blocks formed one of the most concentrated loads ever carried by an aircraft – the container filled with these blocks measured about five feet in length by two feet square and weighed one ton.

Silver City Airways – 1950

With the general awareness by the public of the new ferry service, and it rapidly becoming a popular feat of one-upmanship to airlift ones' car to France, the 1950 season had opened with a new 2½ year associate agreement licence with B.E.A., and an additional service to the motorists in the form of Autocheques Limited. This company, working in conjunction with Silver City, provided a Continental-wide service by recommending hotels, reserving shipping space, issuing touring documents, despatching any spare parts needed for repairs and making travel currency arrangements.

At this time, to keep pace with the increased volume of traffic, Silver City then designed a new 2 hp J.A.P-powered 'Mechanical Moke' loading ramp, of which four were to be used at each terminal to aid loading and speed the turnaround time. Using the John A Priestley engine the first ramps were built locally by the Hythe Engineering Company and called the 'H.E.C', but notwithstanding this advancement the aircraft utilisation rate, which seldom exceeded three hours per day for each aircraft – the equivalent of nine single journeys – was giving cause for concern.

The rates charged to the car owner for a single journey, still £32 for cars over 14'-0" in length and £27 for those shorter (inclusive of all passengers), could not be reduced due allegedly to the extremely high fees charged by the airport authorities. As well as the 35 gallons of petrol needed to complete the 20 minute flight across the Channel, landing fees at Lympne were £7 (but only £4 at Le Touquet), which caused Silver City to repeatedly appeal to the Ministry of Civil Aviation to reduce the landing fees at Lympne, these already totaling nearly £1000 per week during the peak summer period.

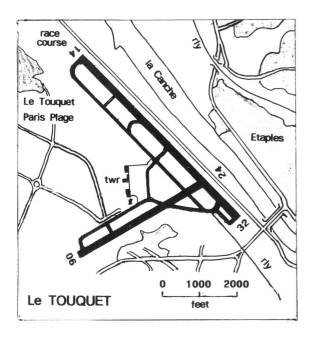

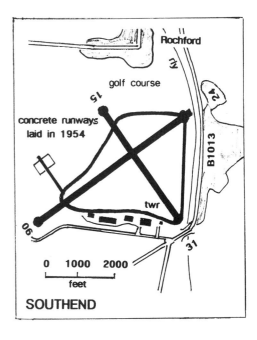

In 1949/50 the M.C.A. had granted reductions of 80% on landing fees for scheduled flights between UK destinations no greater than 40 miles apart, with a 60% reduction on those between 41 and 80 miles, and halved landing fees for scheduled flights between 81 and 115 miles, but because the route between Lympne and Le Touquet was international the M.C.A. rightly stated that these subsidies did not apply. Silver City then pointed out (albeit to no avail) that these fees represented about £16 for every hour flown, or approximately 25% of their normal operating costs, and that these costs were swollen by a 5d per gallon increase in petrol at the end of 1949. The only concession made by the M.C.A. was to allow Silver City to improve their facilities at Lympne in order to encourage more flights, and therefore earn even more revenue in landing fees.....

Despite the company's continuing conflict with the M.C.A. the 1950 season had started on a more lighter note. In January, no doubt in order to demonstrate that a vintage car could withstand the rigors of a channel crossing by air, and also to show the flexibility of the service, a sample flight was set up between Lympne and Le Touquet. This consisted of one Freighter carrying a 1904 Darracq and a 1950 Austin A70, with a second Freighter flying a parallel course with a 1950 Alvis en route to the Amsterdam Motor Show.

One improvement made to Freighters employed on the car ferry services was to have the nose door strutting modified slightly so as to give a two foot increase in the hold length. By routing the strutting around the edges of the door it was found possible to put the last loaded vehicle slightly more forward than normal, thus giving the chance to take more of the larger vehicles that were using the service.

Silver City Airways - 1951

The 1951 season opened in good form when in March a new agent, Instone Air Transport, was appointed. Additionally, for the first time, Silver City rationalised their fare structure, the single fares being revised in the spring as follows: £16 for cars up to 12'-6", £20 for 12'-6" to 15'-0", and £24 for 15'-6" and over. Motor cycles were £3, motorcycle (sidecar) combinations £5, bicycles £1 and passengers £2.

To demonstrate what effect this had, in May bookings were up 400% on the 1950 figures, and in July alone a total of six Freighters made 42 round trips carrying over 80 cars, 75 motor cycles, 65 bicycles and 411 passengers. Also in August the cargo figure lifted and set down at Lympne was more than 2½ times the combined totals of all cargo handled at London Airport and Northolt. This total, at 4,047 short tons, was only 27 tons below the total freight handled at all the U.K. aerodromes during August of 1950.

In 1951 the Silver City Freighter fleet increased to seven, with G-AICM acquired from Hunting Aerosurveys in May and F-BEND & 'ENH from Cie Air Transport in November. In 1950 C.A.T. and their associate companies had six Freighters until F-BENF, a Mk 21, crashed in the Sahara 90 miles from Alouet on 28 July. This mishap aside, their record for that year had been good with operations for both charter and scheduled services totalling 4,425 tons of freight and 37,350 passengers, but as trade slowed part of the fleet was put up for disposal and a third Freighter, F-BECT, was passed to Silver City in April 1952.

Involvement by Silver City in the Berlin Airlift was resumed in September of the 1951/52 season, when two Freighters started a term of unscheduled freight movements by flying blockaded exports out of Berlin to the German port of Hamburg. This had restarted due to a Russian demand for new consignment forms for both road and rail transport through the 100-mile strip of East German territory separating Berlin from the West. During the first twelve months of this operation the two aircraft flew approximately 305,000 aircraft miles, the equivalent of 900,000 revenue miles, carrying 5,500 tons of freight on 1050 trips over the 152-mile stage between Templehof and Hamburg. At the end of the first 16 months of the airlift a total of 35,000 tons of industrial goods produced in Berlin worth 340M Marks (about £28m) had been flown to West Germany.

A number of other events happened that are worth recording. In November Silver City was given one of the largest cattle contracts of its kind ever awarded in this country up to that time, entailing shipping over 1,800 cows across the Channel en route from Ireland to Italy. To contain the cattle special 'aerial pens' were constructed in the aircraft holds and allowed between eight to eleven animals, a load of approximately 9850 lbs, to be carried. With the intention of a Freighter taking off every 90 minutes during daylight hours, the cattle were to be transported at the rate of 300 head per week over a period of six consecutive weeks but, unfortunately for Silver City, it was not to be as simple as it had at first seemed.

The contract actually commenced at the beginning of 1952 but, due to recent bad weather conditions, the grass runways at Lympne were so seriously affected by waterlogging that they were declared unserviceable, and the usable payload for the Freighter limited to only 8,000lbs. Silver City even offered the M.C.A. cash as part payment towards putting things right, but were forced to conclude the contract by flying the cattle out from Blackbushe, Southend and West Malling. The end result was a loss per trip of around £500, a fact that must have been more than just irritating, especially when considering that in 1951 company aircraft had contributed to 85% of the movements at Lympne and consequently paid nearly £20,000 in landing fees to the M.C.A.

In October Silver City had been granted an additional associate agreement licence to operate a 35 minute vehicle ferry service over the 88 mile route between Southampton (Eastleigh) and Cherbourg (Maupertus), but as the French authorities were slow to install the required navigational aids the formalities were not complete until 5 December when a demonstration flight was undertaken. Amongst the passengers on this first flight were the Lady Mayor of Southampton, Councillor M Cutler OBE, and the Eastleigh Mayor, Councillor T E Stubbs, who were received on arrival by the Mayor of Cherbourg. Single carriage rates for the new service (supposed to have been inaugurated on a scheduled basis on 10 January 1952 but commenced on 1 February for the reasons given above) were as follows:- cars up to 12'-0" £15, 12'-0" to 13'-6" £19, 13'-6" to 15'-6" £23, and over 15'-6" £27. Motorcycles were £5, motorcycle combinations £7, autocycles £2-10s, bicycles £1-5s, and each passenger £4.

Silver City Airways - 1952

Also in November 1951 Silver City had been granted a further ten year associate agreement licence to continue the Lympne to Le Touquet vehicle ferry service. The agreement, which took effect on 31 December 1951, was the longest licence ever granted by the Ministry and coincided with an invitation from the Municipal Authorities at Southend for Silver City to start a vehicle ferry service from Southend Airport.

Being duly impressed with the facilities at Southend, the feasibility of such a route was demonstrated on 30 January when a Freighter was flown to Brussels, followed the next day by a second trip from Southend to Ostende. The object of this exercise was to give Belgian officials, travel agents, and members of the press a preview of the proposed daily 99-mile vehicle ferry service between Southend and Middlekerke Airport. The service proper was initially scheduled to start on an experimental basis on 10 April but did not not get going until 14 April when a Freighter Mk 21 carried as its cargo one car and five passengers. It was, however, to be very short-lived.

Although the route sector to Middlekerke was longer than that on the Southend to Cherbourg service Silver City had decided to charge identical carriage rates, this having arisen from a Southend Municipal Authority ruling that, in order to encourage more trade, regular users of its airport would be charged cheaper airfield fees than was normal at M.C.A. aerodromes. However, and within only a matter of a few days of being inaugurated, the operation was found to be uneconomical due to an unexpected lack of patrons, and was never resumed on a scheduled basis except on occasions when Lympne became flooded. Southend was thus used as a substitute airfield for all the Lympne services with the Ostende service only carried out from Lympne on an on-demand basis.

March saw, amongst other things, the purchase by Britavia Limited of the entire £26,000 share capital of Aquila Airways Limited, Britain's last commercial flying boat operator – a purchase that was obviously attributed to Air Commodore Powell's love of flying boats. Aquila had been formed in May 1948 by Wing Commander Brian Aikman and commenced operations after purchasing ex-Corporation Hythes and by 1952, with one Solent delivered and three more on order, it extended its Madeira and Lisbon services (inaugurated in May 1949) to Las Palmas. The company also did a limited amount of charter work, of which the most notable was the 1951 evacuation of Anglo-Iranian oil staff from Basra.

Silver City were also approved in March to operate a scheduled 120-mile vehicle ferry and freight service between Southampton and Guernsey and/or Jersey. The licence was granted for seven years with but one proviso, this being that the number of passengers carried per flight was not to exceed three, so as to safeguard the existing Channel Island Airlines. This ruling eventually forced the company to postpone, at least temporarily, its plans to start this service because of Air Transport Advisory Council non-approval to allow a minimum of six passengers, BEA being the only objectors on the basis of this approval.

A bone of contention for some time was the fact that, under the terms of the licence for the cross-Channel services, passengers travelling without a vehicle could not be carried. To get round this ruling it was arranged that a stock of bicycles be kept at both Lympne and at Le Touquet, thus foot passengers could turn up, collect a cycle and board the aircraft with it, thereby 'accompanying a vehicle'. Whilst this arrangement worked it did not amuse one maintenance worker at Lympne who finished his shift only to find his transport home had been borrowed by a passenger and was now residing at Le Touquet!

Generally 1952 saw Silver City involved in the shipment of a number of odd cargoes. In the summer period more than 20 pigeon charters were received from various international pigeon organisations who raced their birds between the UK and the Continent, and between January and July, 233 British, French and Irish racehorses were carried, but the strangest animal charter was the ferrying of a number of stags and two does in fawn. These were being delivered, so to speak, to Germany as replacements for those destroyed in the area around Grunewald during the Second World War.

Other tasks by Silver City included airlifting the entire contents of all 212 rooms at the North Atlantic Treaty Organisation headquarters in London from Lympne to Cormeilles, and required three aircraft to work continuously over the course of a single weekend in April to move 90 tons of freight. Another was a trip on 16 May between Southampton and Cherbourg. Nothing very unusual about this, particularly as the company had the licence to operate on this route, except it was quoted that history was made in coordinating land, sea and air transport when a medium sized car plus a 12ft racing dinghy were carried (the cost of transporting the boat being £15 for the single journey).

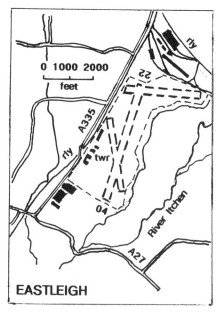

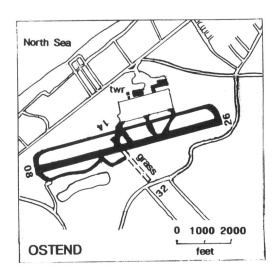

Following a decision back in November 1951 by Cream Cheese Limited of Southampton to use air transport instead of surface shipping, Silver City were to become involved in what came to be known as the 'Cream Cheese Specials'. The Southampton company had for some time been aware that the extra two days the air service would give them would prolong the selling life of their cheese, thus enhancing its sales in the North of England and Scotland. This reasoning, also by part, strengthened Silver City's endeavour to expand its future goods services by coordinating them with road transport on each side of the Channel and thus advertised its Freighter availability for hire at a one-way charter fee of just £55.

Nevertheless, as to the cream cheese charters, every Sunday morning at least one of the company's Freighters would meet a fleet of large refrigerated lorries at Le Touquet and take on approximately 5 tons of expensive and perishable Pommel, Gervaise, Lion Rouge and Napoleon Camembert cheeses to be flown to Lympne. From here they were distributed around the country, and in the first year of operation the Freighters made a total of 127 such flights. Silver City also carried a limited amount of French cheeses from Cherbourg to Southampton on behalf of L'Industrie Laitiere de Normandie et du Cotentin, of Bricquebec, but as these consignments only amounted to about 500 lbs per week they were flown on the regular scheduled services.

Apart than a brief report in April that Silver City planned to start a vehicle ferry service between Southampton and the Isle of Wight, there was only one other operation envisaged. This was a limited vehicle ferry service between Blackpool (Squires Gate) and the Isle of Man, carrying cars with accompanying passengers, motorcycles and bicycles during the two or three days immediately before and after the TT races. The service would have been run in conjunction with the Lancashire Aircraft Corporation, who were to be responsible for servicing the Freighters at Squires Gate, but did not however take place. Whilst rates for the service were fairly reasonable at - small car £13, large car £21, motorcycles £4-10s, bicycles £1, and passengers accompanying cars £4-5s, Silver City believed that the service would be too expensive to set up and it was therefore shelved.

Referring to operations by Silver City in 1952, their nine Freighters had completed more than one million miles of flying, the millionth mile actually being flown on 31 December, and to achieve this their aircraft had taken off and landed over 9,000 times without mishap. However, during the year, their air ferry division carried about 10% less traffic than in 1951, but needless to say this did not heed the 100,000th car being carried on 1 July. This was, by chance, a Rolls-Royce owned by Sir Charles Lloyd Jones, chairman of a large Australian department store who happened to be on holiday in Europe at this time.

The provisional statistics shown below were published by Silver City at the close of the 1952 season, and had been 'rounded off' for presentation-

	All divisions	Air Ferry division	Berlin and charter division
Miles flown	1,000,050	301,000	699,050
Passengers carried	28,500	27,000	1,500
Cars carried	7,000	6,970	30
Motorcycles carried	2,200	2,200	–
Bicycles carried	1,850	1,850	–
Freight in tons (including vehicles)	21,000	12,250	8,750
Total fleet flying time (hours)	7,000	–	–
Equivalent annual utilisation per aircraft (hours)	825	–	–

The company also published for the first time their seasonal profits, which for 1951 and 1952 were £47,478 and £35,094 respectively.

At the end of 1952 there were a number of reports stating that Silver City had been granted concessions by the Kingdom of Libya to operate a freight and passenger service between the two capitals of Benghazi and Tripoli. Against strong opposition from Egyptian, Italian and American operators the agreement had been the outcome of lengthy discussions between Libya's Ministry of Communications, the Director of Civil Aviation and Silver City, and was expected to begin in January 1953. Under terms of the agreement Silver City was contracted to form a new organisation within twelve months with the majority holding by Libyan subjects, and in fact the Anglo-Libyan Bilateral Civil Air Service agreement was signed in Tripoli on Saturday 21 February 1953.

Silver City's involvement in this scheme had originally stemmed from an article that Air Commodore Powell had read in 'The Times', placed in that paper in October by the Libyan Government who wanted a company to run an internal air service in their country. They described the difficulties arising from the fact that Libya had two capitals whereby, due to the insistence of King Idris that Benghazi be the capital, and a similar insistence by his Parliament that Tripoli be the main city, the opportunity to start this unique airline would probably not have arisen. Neither the King nor his subjects would give way, and so there was a compromise – two capitals, 416 miles apart as the crow (or aeroplane) flies. As a result, the demand for transport between the two cities (particularly when considering that the countries' court held a six-monthly session at each capital) was agitated not only by the indirectness of the 36-hour, 660-mile overland journey between them but also by the profile of the coastline with its infrequent shipping services.

Silver City Airways – 1953

This year saw an accident to one of Silver City's Freighters working on the Berlin Airlift. On 19 January G-AICM, a Mk 21, took off from Templehof with a cargo comprising three drums of cable bound for Hamburg but on arrival there found the airfield obscured by fog. After circling for twenty minutes the Captain decided to divert to Bremen, but found this also fog-bound so returned to Templehof for a GCA landing. Unfortunately the Templehof ground equipment became unserviceable and, after flying around for some time to use up the remaining fuel, the aircraft was eventually force-landed under very restricted conditions on railway lines. In the resulting crash, when the aircraft lost both wings, the tailplane, its undercarriage and one of the cable drums which broke its way out, no-one was hurt but the aircraft was so badly damaged that it was reduced to produce.

The enquiry hearing determined that the crash had resulted from the Captain having failed to ensure that sufficient fuel was on board, and for the first time Silver City were found negligent in the operation of an aircraft. Accordingly they were fined £200 with 40 guineas costs and the Captain was fined £50. The company was further fined £20, and the Captain £10, for failing to carry a co-pilot.

After preliminaries in December 1952, and the establishment of operational headquarters at both capitals, the first scheduled Libyan Airways service on the new 2½-hour, 416-mile direct route was inaugurated on 1 February 1953. Bristol Freighter Mk 21 G-AIFM flew a number of passengers, a Morris Minor car (previously shipped out from Blackbushe in one of the Mk 21s), and over a ton of mail between Idris-el-Awal airfield, Tripoli and Benina airfield, Benghazi, but arrived some two hours late due to the enthusiasm of onlookers at Tripoli. For this service, operated once a day in each direction by one of two Silver City Freighters, G-AIFM and 'IFV, the aircraft were flown in Libyan Airways' colours with tiny lettering 'Operated by Silver City Airways' over just the rear exit door. On the forward nose doors in bright colours was the new insignia of the Libyan Kingdom, with the words 'Libyan Airways' in large letters on each fuselage side.

It was not the intention of Silver City to compete with the existing international trucking operators on this route, and this necessitated their trade being drawn mainly from local surface transportation. This trade usually consisted of goats, horses, sheep, cattle, motor

Silver City Airways Freighter Mk 21 G-AGHJ at Palam airfield, Delhi, during the Partition of India operations in August 1947 (photo by Jack Roberts, Mold, Flintshire).

Silver City Airways Freighter Mk 21 G-AGVC 'City of Sheffield', the first in service with nose loading doors, outside the maintenance hangar at Lympne (SCA photo).

SCA Freighter Mk 21 G-AIFV at Blackbushe in December 1952 wearing the colour scheme of Libyan Airways for its forthcoming role in North Africa (SCA photo).

The car park for the booking office at Lympne, adequate in size for the time. What the policeman (centre) was required for, or the identity of the prominent lady, is not known. The 'temporary' wartime nature of the airfield buildings is apparent in this shot (SCA photo).

Cyclists and other passengers outside the Silver City Airways reception area at Lympne. The low building with the verandah this side of the dark one with chimneys is the original booking office with the car park at rear, the one on the right is the Meteorological Office (who knocked the post over?). These buildings continued to deal with 'Lympne' services when the split Lympne/Lydd system was set up prior to Ferryfield opening (SCA photo).

Not all cars carried had happy holidaymakers in, this one at Lympne was typical of the many insurance recoveries after Continental accidents (photo via Arthur Leftley, Westcliff, Essex).

The SCA reception hall and car park for 'Lydd' services in the tented 'city' at Lympne from July to October 1954 (SCA photo).

Ferryfield terminal buildings under construction early in 1954, viewed from midway along runway 04/22 near to its intersection with runway 14/32 (SCA photo).

vehicles and general freight which, when added to the nine second and twenty third class passengers that could be accommodated in the standard configuration, gave the company a tremendous scope for potential consignments however, when fitted out in the all-passenger configuration, forty-two third-class could be carried. Solely first class accommodation was not necessary since the operation was not aimed at the existing international airline traffic.

Second class passengers paid £10 single and £15 return fares for the journey, and were seated in a separate nine-place rear cabin in the Freighter whilst the twenty travelling third class were accommodated behind a moveable bulkhead in the centre of the aircraft, all being without soundproofing, at £6 single and £11 return. Space remaining allowed for stowage of 6,000 lbs of freight, but if the aircraft was used solely for livestock freight, up to five horses or camels, 12 head of cattle, or 40 sheep and goats could be carried. Single fare rates for the animals were:- horses and camels £24, cattle £12, sheep and goats £4.

As to the animals carried, the first ever consignment flown during February was a three-year old pedigree cow and four-week old calves. The same month also saw the first flock of 110 sheep being flown between the two cities, such was the exhilaration of this flight that it was reported they positively revelled in the joys of flying - so much in fact as to cause the last few out to make a six-foot jump to the ground instead of using the ramp!

With the consolidation of the Tripoli and Benghazi service the intention was also to provide flights to Sebha in the southern province of Fezzan, and the Oasis of Kufra in Cyrenaica, followed by services to Egypt and Tunisia, and the possible carriage of pilgrims to Mecca. There was also talk of special flights for the benefit of the British garrison in Tripoli and the flying of troops to both Malta and Tunis during their leave period, fares for the 239-mile return journey to Malta being £6, and for the 338-mile return journey to Tunis £10.

The first of these charters went out on the last Saturday in February, when a flight to Malta carried no fewer than 42 American passengers for a visit to personnel of Patrol Squadron 8, United States Air Detachment at Luqa. Piloted by Captain J Wilson and with a Libyan steward on board the Freighter, G-AIFM, touched down at Luqa airfield to much speculation that the flight had the largest consignment of passengers ever to leave Tripoli on one aircraft.

March also saw other charters organised, Libyan government officials were carried on a four-hour, each-way trip to Kufra Oasis, and the first air tour from Tripoli to Jerusalem was arranged so that 36 passengers could leave on Good Friday and spend Easter in the Holy Land. This trip was to return the following Wednesday after night stops in Cairo on the outward journey and Beirut on the return. No refreshments were served on these runs, but on one the crew were surprised to be brought fresh cups of tea by passengers, and on going back to find out how these drinks were being prepared, found some of the pilgrims happily clustered round a kettle suspended over a fire built directly onto the aircraft floor!

However, in the end, although it is true to say that Silver City went to great lengths to satisfy the area's needs, and there was even talk of complementing the Freighters with all-passenger Dakotas, objections to the services eventually stemmed from the airlines enforced competition with BEA. Even though BEA's inter-capital rates were in the region of 50% higher than Libyan Airways, Libyan subjects tended to be drawn towards the BEA service, operated with Elizabethans, because food and drink was served between the two capitals. Thus, after a short time, Silver City's involvement in the Airline ceased after it was found to be almost impossible to implement the service, in spite of the King of Libya's decree that all Libyan subjects should use the state airline where possible. In the end Silver City's last operatives pulled out of Libya on 17 June 1954, after being involved in the operation since 15 December 1952.

On the home front, January 1953 had seen new rates announced by Silver City for their Lympne to Le Touquet service with effect from 1 April. These involved reductions of up to 75% on their 1952 charges, these rates having originally been submitted to the M.C.A. on 14 August 1952, which are shown in the following table:-

Type of vehicle	1953 rate	1952 rate
Bicycle	5s	£1-0s
Bicycle with clip motor	5s	£2-0s
Scooter	£1-5s	£4-0s
Motorcycle under 250cc	£1-15s	£4-0s
Motorcycle over 250cc	£2-10s	£4-0s
Motorcycle combination	£3-10s	£6-0s
Cars up to 12ft 6ins	£7-10s	£16-0s
Cars between 12ft 6ins and 13ft 6ins	£10-0s	£16-0s
Cars between 13ft 6ins and 14ft 6ins	£12-10s	£20-0s
Cars between 14ft 6ins and 15ft 6ins	£15-0s	£20-0s
Cars between 15ft 6ins and 16ft 6ins	£17-10s	£24-0s
Cars over 16ft 6ins	£20-0s	£24-0s
Passengers accompanying vehicles	£2-0s	£2-5s
Other passengers	£2-5s	---

(in all cases the return fare was double the single rate shown)

Fare reductions also applied from Southampton to Cherbourg as well as on the 'on-demand' Lympne to Ostende route, which had replaced the ill-fated Southend to Ostende service. The rates to both Cherbourg and Ostende were also revised to exactly £3 more than the relative car category as shown in the table above, and the effect these revisions had was quickly reflected in the number of advance bookings received by February.

Over January and February the booking figures for vehicles were 3,719 for cars, 2,225 for motorcycles and 360 for cycles, compared with 507, 532 and 34 respectively for the same period in 1952. This was an effective percentage increase of some 633% for cars, 318% for motorcycles and 958% for cycles, while the booking increase for the week ending 28 February, when compared with the same week in 1952, showed an increase of 879% in car bookings and 740% for motorcycles.

Silver City's plans for the 1953 season were designed primarily around the purchase of six extended Freighter aircraft - the Mk 32 Superfreighter. The first of these, G-AMWA, was delivered on 31 March (when pilot Jim Broadbent snagged the Lympne boundary fence with its tailwheel) and the last on 23 June. These aircraft, described more fully in Appendices 2 & 3, and listed in Appendix 9, first appeared in operation over Easter when G-AMWA went into service on the Lympne to Le Touquet route.

In March Silver City received approval to operate a further three vehicle ferry services:-
    1) London (Gatwick) to Le Touquet (ten years),
    2) Southend and/or Lympne to Ostende (seven years),
    3) Southampton (Eastleigh) to Bembridge (IoW) (ten years).

Thus five routes were scheduled for operation by the company, as shown in Appendix 4.

The proving flight for the first of these, the 91-mile route from Gatwick with its rail link from Victoria railway station, was undertaken on 15 April when Captain Len Madelaine took Superfreighter G-AMWB with ten pressmen, Air Commodore Powell, Mr W G Franklin, Sir Alfred le Maitre (controller of ground services for the Ministry of Civil Aviation), Mr E Manley Walker, the route manager for Silver City, and three new Austin A30 cars for export, to Le Touquet. The journey, which started from Victoria at 11.28, took one hour 39 minutes and concluded with the party being met on arrival at the French terminal by its director, M Sainsard and the town mayor, Dr Pouget, before being conducted to a civil function and returning to Gatwick the same day.

The service proper was inaugurated to the public on 15 May, and for consistency on this planned twice-daily schedule it was decided to charge the same vehicle rates as those for the Cherbourg route, except that passengers paid £4 single and £7-4s return fares.

Whilst the second of these approvals was to enable the company to consolidate the existing Lympne to Ostende vehicle ferry operation the third service, Eastleigh to Bembridge, was a different proposition. It had been hoped to start this route on 2 April but, after a detailed assessment of the ground conditions at Bembridge, it was agreed to wait until 15 May in order to give the authorities time to extend the main grass runway to 4250 ft and thus meet the minimum requirements Silver City felt were necessary to receive an aircraft the size of a Freighter. Additionally, a windmill sited on a hill just to the north-east of the airfield was a possible hazard in IMC. However, poor weather during the construction phase delayed the works and despite sterling efforts to complete them in time Silver City, who had visualised operating 12 return flights per day on this 21-mile, 9-minute run, which they dubbed 'the world's shortest passenger and ferry airline service', were again forced to delay its start.

In actual fact, this latter disappointment was received as welcome news by British Railways, who insisted that they were still providing, as they always had done, adequate facilities for coping with all traffic. This view was expressed strongly by British Railways, along with their belief that an air ferry service was unnecessary, when Silver City first applied for a licence to run the service.

Finally Silver City came through when, on the evening of 2 July, an inaugural flight from Eastleigh to Bembridge was flown. Earlier that day a Mk 21 Freighter had made a trial run without cargo but the inaugural carried twelve passengers, including company officials, a Melbourne fashion model, the wife of the Lyndhurst Police Superintendant and reporters, as well as a token load of two cars and a scooter. Reports at the time stated that on the evening of the flight there was not a breath of wind in the air, but after the aircraft had made a perfect landing back at Eastleigh it suffered what can only be attributed to extreme bad luck. The pilot, Captain George Hogarth, had finished his run and taxied up to the far end of the aerodrome but whilst turning to park the starboard main wheel became bogged in down to the axle in a soft patch of ground where a hedge had been removed. Strangely enough, the incident occurred at <u>thirteen</u> minutes past six, but within minutes airfield staff had released the wheel and towed the aircraft clear.

The following day the service was officially opened to the public and although it was run from the beginning of July on an on-demand basis the ABC World Airways Guide had it listed as a scheduled service. When operating the rates for single fares would have been:-
Bicycles 3s, tandems 5s, bicycle with clip motor 7s-6d, motorcycles & scooters 17s-6d, motorcycle combinations £1-5s; cars up to 12'-6" £3-2s-6d, 12'-6" to 13'-6" £3-17s-6d, 13'-6" to 14'-6" £4-12s-6d, 14'-6" to 15'-6" £5-7s-6d, 15'-6" to 16'-6" £6-2s-6d, over 16'-6" £6-17s-6d, and passengers 13s-6d. Freight charges were ¾d per lb with reductions for quantity and special commodities.

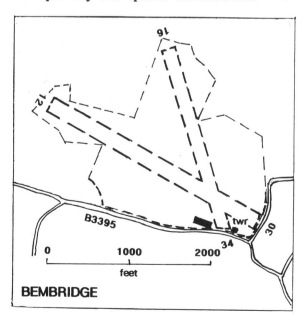

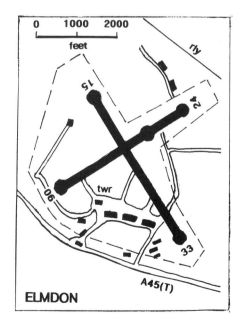

In August, just one month after commencing operations, Silver City then stated they would be suspending the service until the following spring, a decision brought about mainly by the continued bad weather that had delayed the construction of new facilities at Bembridge. Any continuation of this service was eventually cancelled after the Bembridge runway was deemed unsuitable for handling loaded aircraft of Freighter size, even though in January 1954 the company had applied to use Ryde Airport as an alternative to Bembridge, and operate DC3s and DH89s as well as the Freighter. One other factor concerning the use of Bembridge was that, after receiving a telephone call from Eastleigh that a Freighter was inbound, the airport manager Bob McRae, had only minutes to grab a cycle and pedal frantically around the field in order to clear any sheep grazing on the runway!!

It was only in the late 1970s that the runway situation at Bembridge improved, after the Brittan-Norman company set up their Islander production line there, and amalgamation with Pilatus brought about a new concrete runway being laid. With the Brittan-Norman facility sited on the north-east side of the airfield, the existing hangars on the south side were retained and a public house called 'The Propellor' was built. At its peak the BN facility had some 100 workers, who used this public house and in the early days collected their wages from the bar area.

Silver City's first Superfreighter, G-AMWA, had made the news on 6 May when, in order to demonstrate the practicability of a long distance vehicle ferry operation, a 210-mile, 90 minute demonstration flight was set up between Birmingham (Elmdon) and Le Touquet. Arranged by the Automobile Association the flight carried a full complement of passengers, two motorcycles and two cars, and had taken place after the A.A. had estimated that of their 1,250,000 members some 70,000 would be travelling abroad during the year, and that over 20,000 lived within easy reach of Birmingham airport (in 1952 the AA had arranged for over 49,000 of its members to take their vehicles to the Continent). Silver City stated that the single journey to Le Touquet would cost between £30-50 for a medium-sized car and four passengers, depending on the number of people using the service, but whilst the A.A. subsequently sent out questionnaires to all its members asking if this sort of vehicle ferry service was attractive to them, there was only a faint hint of encouragement and the service proper did not materialize until 1955.

As a slight digression, echoes of the earlier Britavia days were evident on 9 May when, under an arrangement with the English Electric company whereby they delivered the first two of a batch of Canberra jet bombers to Venezuela, two of Silver City's pilots set up a joint Trans-Atlantic air speed record from East to West. The pilots, Captains 'Johnnie' Hackett and Robert Damon, flew the first leg of 2260 miles from Warton, Lancashire to Gander, Newfoundland at an average speed of 492 mph, and the second leg from Baltimore to Jamaica achieved an average speed of 530.7 mph.

Sunday, 5 June saw Captain Hackett set another unofficial East to West Trans-Atlantic record when the Canberra he was piloting covered the Warton to Gander leg in four hours and twenty-six minutes, an average speed of 510 mph. This flight was just three days after he had attempted to take another Canberra, carrying some of the first movie films of the Coronation for screening on American and Canadian television, to a touchdown point in Newfoundland but had to turn back due to a fault in the fuel pump actuator circuit.

The official East to West Trans-Atlantic record at this time was still the 483.91 mph, four hours 18 minutes 24.4 seconds flight set on 31 August 1951 by Wing Commander Roland Beaumont, chief test pilot of English Electric, while flying a Canberra between Aldergrove and Gander - a distance of 2072.04 miles.

Another notable flight took place on 14 July with a further Canberra delivery to Venezuela, again piloted by Johnnie Hackett but accompanied by Navigation Officer D J Moneypenny. After leaving Warton at 0352 GMT the aircraft was over Caracus at 1905 that same day, times for the three legs being four hours 46 minutes to Gander, two hours 50 minutes to Baltimore, and four hours 42 minutes to Caracus.

Hackett and Moneypenny would be in the news again on 23 August 1955 when they flew a Canberra PR7, WT528, fitted with a B2 nose, from London to New York and back in one day, and in so doing broke an existing record and set two new ones. After taking off from London Airport at 0710 BST the flight times were recorded by observers from the Royal Aero Club on behalf of the International Aeronautical Federation and logged as follows:- Over Croydon 0717, over Gander 1225, landed at Floyd Bennett Naval Airfield, New York 1448. Left New York 1523, over Croydon 2141, and landed at London Airport 2151 hrs.

Official figures for the 3457.96-mile outward flight between Croydon and New York were seven hours 29 minutes 56.7 seconds, at an average speed of 461.12 mph, with the return flight of six hours 16 minutes 59.5 seconds producing an average speed of 550.35 mph. The Croydon to Croydon time was fourteen hours 21 minutes 45.4 seconds, which included the 35 minute turn-round at New York, and returned a reported average speed of 481.52 mph although this was eventually confirmed as 481.935 mph.

Up to this time the only comparable records for the crossing had been the unofficial time set three years previous by a Pan American Airways pilot, Captain Charles Blair who, by flying a North American Mustang between New York and London, took seven hours 35 minutes. The previous official time for this West to East crossing, 20 hours 29 minutes, was set in 1937 by Henry Merrill and John Landes in a Lockheed Electra.

While the above figures may seem rather insignificant when compared with the deed, this record-breaking trend was rather near to the heart of one of the company's management. In August 1937 Captain Griffith James Powell (then with Imperial Airways) had set up an unofficial Trans-Atlantic record by piloting the flying boat 'Cumbria' the 2000 miles from Foynes, Ireland to Botwood, Newfoundland in 14 hours 24 minutes, just three minutes more than it had taken 'his boys' to do the round trip 16 years later.

Returning to Silver City....... other vehicular activities during 1953 included the carriage of the first cars ever to be flown into Belgium for export, when three Austin family saloons were delivered to Ostende on 20 June, and on 30 August a Wolselely 4/44 and two Morris Minors were the first export models flown into Switzerland in one of the Mk 32s routed via Lympne to Zurich. Previously in March, several Standard Motor Company cars had been flown from Lympne to Geneva for that city's Motor Show.

These brief excursions into Switzerland and other European destinations later in the year must have prompted Silver City to think of the potential of routinely flying cars there, for on 11 December approval was from the Ministry of Transport to operate a 490-mile, three hour seasonal/winter vehicle ferry between Blackbushe and Kloten Airport, Zurich. This three month experimental service, inaugurated on 2 January 1954, comprised a once-weekly return flight scheduled to leave Blackbushe at 0800 on Saturday mornings and return at 1430 on Sunday. The one way rate for cars over 13'-6" in length was £35, while for those shorter it was £25, passengers were charged £14-17s single and £26-15s return.

Just as Silver City's involvement in the Berlin Airlift was again evident they were initiating searches for a larger aircraft with which to operate the envisaged deep-penetration services into Europe. In 1952 the company had expressed a wish to buy three Blackburn Universal Freighters, but there were some doubts as to whether this large aircraft would materialise in a civil version. Bristol produced many designs, the Type 179 twin-boomed Freighter in 1951, the 179A with twin booms and an upswept rear fuselage in 1952, the Centaurus-engined 179B in 1954, two unusual V/STOL versions of the GOR 351 in 1958, and the Dart-engined 216 (originated jointly with Breguet) which did not materialise until 1959 due to the merger into the BAC. The Handley Page HPR8 and HPR9 car ferries were still in the early design stages, but the first available choice was the dual-deck Avion Louis Breguet 763 'Deux Ponts' which was just commencing production.

Once the formalities were over Breguet agreed to let Silver City experiment with the second of three pre-series type 761S 'Deux Ponts', the first production version of the 763, for a trial period. However, realising that the British air ferry terminals at Gatwick, Lympne and Southampton were incapable of handling the type, it was decided that the best way to amass sufficient costings and other performance-related operational data would be to use it on the Berlin Airlift. Accordingly the aircraft was collected from Toulouse at the beginning of July and, under contract to the Berlin Senate, put into service under the command of Captain C I Hopkins bearing Silver City titles but still retaining its French registration, F-BASL.

Whilst it had been considered that there would be little difficulty in modifying the interior of the 761S to the vehicle ferry configuration, Silver City knew that the aircraft could only be economically viable on such stage lengths as the proposed Birmingham to Le Touquet route, or the even longer projected service to Paris. Nevertheless the Berlin trials proved very useful to Silver City, who calculated that one 761 was equivalent to about 3½ Bristol Freighters, with the capability to carry six cars, three on each deck.

Over the following three months the aircraft flew 240 hours and completed 127 round trips carrying, towards the end of the trials, about 170,000 lbs a day in six trips, returning to Berlin light. One of the most significant revelations was that its fuel consumption was far better than the manufacturers had predicted, the other that it covered the 152-mile stage between Berlin and Hamburg in 52 minutes, compared with 63 minutes previously taken by the Freighters. These and other points impressed Silver City with the potential of the Deux Ponts, but the fate of the designs' eventual vehicle ferry usage was ultimately tied up with its cost which was too high for the company to bear. With the later death of Breguet no further designs came from the company for Silver City to evaluate.

Of the other types considered as eventual aircraft replacement the HPR8 & 9 seemed quite promising. Extensive design studies were finally completed in 1961, in the meantime Silver City had decided merely to acquire more of the Mk 32 Superfreighter, and in a letter to the authors the HP designer John Allan wrote - *"the HPR8 was conceived in collaboration with Hurel-Dubois, who had previously tendered designs to Silver City but recognised the merits of the HPR idea and joined forces. Whilst the French government was willing to put money into the project the British were not so forthcoming. Based on the use of Herald components the engines were Dart RDa 10, takeoff weight was 56,000 lbs with a range of 200 nm, and either 100 passengers or six large cars and 25 passengers could be carried.*

The 11' 0" wide unpressurised fuselage had a honeycomb floor with nothing beneath so it could be hosed down, and cars entered through clamshell doors. It wasn't a pretty aircraft but it had homely appeal, and the rather potty idea of a passenger observation window in the nose to ease looking after birdstrikes during the 150 kt cruise was not wholly daft but caused some comments to be made.

Later we were so enthused with the wide cabin layout that we designed an entirely new aircraft, the HPR9, with twin Speys and prettier lines - still for ultra short haul and 100 passengers plus car capabilities. The twin aisle cabin was a double bubble on its side with the cusps joined by removable posts with a 3.5 psi pressure raised in the passenger side, whilst in the car or freight versions the posts were removable and the aircraft then flown unpressurised. The economics of the type were very good, mostly due to the provision for fast turnround which, on ultra short ranges, was worth a lot of block speed.

Looking back, the project could have been a big success, but Sir Frederick (Handley Page) died in 1962 and Reading was closed, and HM Government was very frosty to HP's".

Returning to 1953, Silver City's Bristol Freighter vehicle ferry operations saw a continued upward trend in the number of vehicles carried. In the first ten months of the year over 38,000 vehicles were uplifted, compared with 10,344 in 1952, this being highlighted at the end of July when, between Friday 31 July and Monday 3 August, their aircraft made 600 channel crossings. On the Saturday 850 vehicles and 2,200 passengers were flown over to France, which resulted from an aircraft taking off and and landing at Lympne every two minutes 18 seconds throughout the operating day.

The company also received a boost to their traffic figures during the French strike from 6–23 August when, during this 17-day period, their aircraft made 1,840 channel crossings carrying in excess of 21,000 passengers, 3,300 cars, 1,800 motorcycles and 1,400 bicycles.

Of the many people that passed over the channel during 1953 there were a few memorable personages. Mr John Lee-Warner left Lympne on the first leg of his estimated five month cycle trip to Australia to be married, a party of five Australian nurses and one man with their 1928 taxi 'Jezebel' flew to the Continent to start a 10,000 mile camping tour, and a rather colourful gent named Alvin Rhiando whose scooter, with its improvised bodywork endorsed with countless trade names, was to carry him to Cape Town, South Africa. Peter Townsend, previously equerry to HM the King, left with his car on a flight to Ostende at the end of his associations with the Princess Margaret when he took up the post of Air Attache in Brussels. Just some of the many dignitaries carried were Sir Bernard and Lady Docker, who frequently travelled with their gold-plated Daimler to the Continent.

Some other well advertised travellers in August were a consignment of 84 Lantras (Swedish Landrace pigs), flown in from Malmo to Cambridge. After experiencing a lack of surface shipping space, and in order to get the pigs into the country for their quarantine period to expire before the coming Peterborough Autumn Sales, it was necessary to fly them in. For this, and future flights of the same nature, special pens were designed by Mr S A Tennant, then the company technical director, incorporating easily assembled and dismantled cubicles which allowed up to 28 animals carried on each flight to be housed separately. For ease of cleaning canvas sheeting covered the freight floor, whilst 'pig netting' was placed over the top of each pen to subdue the animals while in flight. As with all the animals carried it was found that particularly the pigs suffered no ill effects, but to minimise any possible distress the Freighters never exceeded an altitude of 2,000 feet.

The 'Tennant' pens, whilst ideal for the task, did have some failings, such as one instance en route from Cherbourg when an in-foal mare broke the restraining bar and threshed her forelegs out of the pen, causing the pilot to declare an emergency and divert to Eastleigh. When the pens were used for sheep it was found that, with the animals in close proximity to others, the steam arising from them sweating soon misted up the instrument panel and windscreen, thus causing temporary 'blind' flying. Another problem with sheep was their restlessness during flights; on one occasion during a mass moveabout a pen came loose and most of the flock moved to the rear of the Freighter's hold, the resulting change in flight attitude requiring the second pilot to slide <u>down</u> the floor slope and force his way through the sheep before herding them forward again and resecuring the pens.

It was found that a lot of animal litter could build up after the carriage of livestock, and usually the easiest way to clear it from the floor was to hose it away. Unfortunately this method caused other problems inasmuch as the liquid then went into the underfloor area and initiated corrosion of the framework until holes could be drilled to let it drain out. The Freighter was a basic workhorse, but even so the aircrews expected it to be clean enough to perform their daily tasks in. One pilot, an Australian named Jim Broadbent (one of the 1936 England-Australia air race pilots, but later killed in a flying boat accident), became so fastidious about cleanliness that on arrival in the aeroplane, and before starting his spell of duty, he would dust the cockpit, lay a white sheet over his seat, and put toilet paper under the radio headset earpieces so as not to be contaminated by the previous wearer.

On the subject of water penetration into the cockpit – due to the relatively low altitudes the cross-Channel flights operated at (1500' outbound and 850–1000' return), rain and sea spray would inevitably seep in through the cockpit window joins. Cracks in the windshield also let in water, and these were marked with chinagraph by the crews for the maintenance men to pick up. Although we are assured that aircrew were at their stations and attentive throughout every flight, I have been reliably informed that, once the crossword was finished with, 'The Times' was the best way to soak up any intruding water before it got anywhere near the crew seats! Water entry onto the cockpit floor also caused minor corrosion where it joined the rear bulkhead, and many on-site repairs were done to this area during routine maintenance.

Smoking on the flight deck was commonplace, some pilots preferring a pipe whilst others used cigarettes. In the case of the latter, and as the Very pistols fitted in the flight deck roof were gradually withdrawn from use, it was possible to 'magically' dispose of ash by flicking it up to the ceiling where the suction created by the empty flare tube took it away.

Although the Freighters were fitted with a toilet at the rear of the passenger compartment, it was not used very often due to the relatively short flight times (say 20 minutes to Le Touquet), but on the odd occasion when one of the flight crew needed to 'go' it was a case of moving the passengers in the back seat rows to get to it.

Apart from the occasional failure of the engine oil scavenge pump another in-service problem was experienced with the tailwheel, the same design as that used previously on wartime types such as the Bristol Blenheim, Vickers Warwick, Westland Lysander and Whirlwind, and Airspeed Horsa (the nosewheel). After taxying out for takeoff the tailwheel castoring was routinely locked in the straight-ahead position, using an electrically-operated system, and unlocked after landing for taxying onto the pan. When the electric unlock did not withdraw the locking pin after landing, and any use of throttle and brakes failed to cure the problem, the co-pilot's role in freeing it off was to stroll very casually through the passenger area to the rear door, remove the nearby fire axe, jump down onto the runway and repeatedly hit the lock unit with the axe until the pin released. A few words of reassurance were usually given to passengers whilst returning to the cockpit.

Amongst the charters in the first half of 1953 were ten Freighter flights between Blackbushe and Paris with horses and passengers, one from Berlin to Hanover with horses only, one from Southampton to Nantes with racing pigeons, one to Paris from Southampton with exhibition equipment for the Air Show and two in each direction between Blackbushe and Hamburg with cars and passengers. In June five consignments of pigeons were flown into Amsterdam from other European cities, while other pigeon flights included one from Southampton to Bilbao and two from Bovingdon to Luxembourg. Good Friday saw one of the largest holiday airlifts carried out from this country when six Freighters flew 252 Frigidaire Limited workers from Lympne to Le Touquet for an Easter weekend on the Continent.

During this period in time there was one charter whereby one Freighter was used to carry out an aerial photographic survey of 50,000 square miles of the coastlines of Kenya and Tanganyika. The aircraft was chartered by Hunting Aerosurveys but the beneficiary was the D'Arcy Exploration Company, who were looking for deposits on behalf of the Anglo-Iranian and Shell oil companies. The Mk 21 Freighter was commanded by Captain C G Hogarth and based at Port Reitz airport for almost 90 days, but was grounded for all but three due to inclement weather. For this photography to be successful it was necessary for the skies to be completely cloud-free so that no shadows were cast on the ground. A clear sky also allowed the aircraft to fly up to 18,000 feet, thereby reducing any lateral movements of the camera platform caused by turbulance from clouds usually encountered at lower altitudes, and meant a 16 mile wide by 100 mile strip of land could be photographed in one run.

The building of Lydd Airport

By the middle of 1953 Silver City Airways were seriously considering plans to build their own 'ferry field' in the vicinity of Dungeness or Romney Marsh, after it became very clear that the 278-acre State-owned grass airfield at Lympne was inadequate to handle increasing traffic volumes, and that operations there were often interrupted by bad weather conditions and water-logged runways peculiar to its 350 feet elevation. Although Lympne was used by light aircraft for many years, and multitudes of fighters in two World Wars, the fact that it was on a hill, surrounded by roads and a housing estate, meant any useful expansion was out of the question (even when Skyways put down a concrete runway across the middle to prevent laden Dakotas from ploughing through the wet grass areas did not help greatly). It also suffered from sea mists and bad summer fogs, as well as the low cloudbase experienced during the winter periods.

When this bad weather stopped operations it was frustrating, especially so for those living on Romney Marsh who took the crew shuttle down the hill next to the airport and broke out of low cloud straightaway into visibility that was clear as far as Dymchurch. Aircrews were sent home on 'available' until 11 pm and, as very few had telephones or cars in those days, were summoned by telegraph boy to return to the airfield when the weather cleared.

SCA's experience in the area had shown there to be no suitable alternative, nor any former wartime field which might have been rehabilitated. One of the deciding factors in the choice of a site was that it should lie no further from Le Touquet than Lympne was. Nevertheless they decided to first approach the Ministry of Transport and Civil Aviation, after news that the latter were still interested in accepting a reasonable offer from a responsible person or organisation who would be willing to run Lympne under a public users licence.

The idea of purchasing Lympne appealed strongly to Silver City, who had for some time hoped to compliment the ferrying activities there with those proposed for their new airport, however, the idea of using two airports in close proximity was considered by many cynical observers as only half-serious and designed to force the hand of the Ministry in the matter of the future of Lympne. It therefore came as no surprise when Silver City found the same opposition as they had experienced back in 1950, when they first offered to buy the site.

The Ministry, who had taken Lympne over as a Customs aerodrome in January 1946, had followed the announcement of a £17,000 loss in 1948 with its intention to dispose of the site for roughly £20,000, but at that time Silver City's ferrying activities were still in the experimental stage and they were therefore reluctant to accept the offer. When in 1950 the company reconsidered the purchase as worthwhile, the Ministry had changed their minds on selling because, for the first time, the revenue gained through Silver City's operations had made it worthwhile keeping the airfield. Whilst on one hand the Ministry wanted Lympne to be profitable, on the other they continually refused to make any improvements to its facilities in order to allow Silver City to fully utilise its potential.

It therefore followed that the company had thoughts of abandoning operations there unless the Ministry made repairs, or reduced the landing fees, or handed it over to them so that at least £30,000 could be immediately spent on repairs, and a further £100,000 during the year. When none of these alternatives were upcoming Silver City again resorted to appealing to the

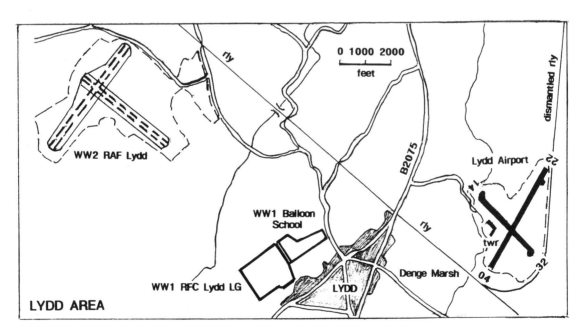

All four flying sites in the Lydd area. L-R the Second World War forward landing ground, the First World War LG, the First World War Balloon School, and the current airport.

Ministry with a view to buying the airfield outright but on all occasions they were balked by ministerial indecision, presumably because of opposition to the deal by the only other resident operator, Air Kruise (Kent) Ltd. The only concession offered by the Ministry had occurred in 1952, after protests were made about the 5/- 'head' tax on passengers, when the landing fees for short-haul flights were reduced, this having the effect of reducing the fees paid by Silver City that year to £12,000.

By 1953, and the Ministry's change of heart, Silver City had stated quite categorically that because of the estimated £150,000 needed above and beyond the purchase price to convert Lympne into an all-weather, all-year operation, they would only be prepared to buy it if the MTCA gave them a realistic purchasing price, presumably similar to the latter's quote of 1949. However the Ministry, for their part, were only willing to base Lympne's value on a direct comparison with the landing fees paid there with the success of Silver City's vehicle ferry operations.

With negotiations seemingly at deadlock the company's doubts about the purchase were finally expounded when it was learnt firstly that Hythe and Folkestone Councils, who had originally turned down the offer to buy the land in 1949, had been considering the idea for some months but declined the offer again. Also, because of the intention to go ahead with their own airport, Lympne would be offered for sale by public auction on 29 April 1953. At the auction however, the Ministry subsequently failed to gain a bid beyond their reserve price. This figure, reputed to have been in the region of £120,000 to £150,000 but was in fact only £90,000, was clearly based on Lympne's value as an airport capable of demanding £20,000 annually in landing fees and not its value as agricultural land, which was estimated to be no greater than £20,000. The Ministry had hoped to sell it for around £100,000.

It could be seen by many that it would have been more logical for the Ministry to have fixed a lower reserve price at the auction, they having realised that the value of Lympne would decrease proportionately with the development of Silver City's new site, and that therefore made the formers stand illogical. As it turned out, the Ministry finally closed Lympne to traffic on 31 October 1954 and sold the land in July 1955 to Mr J M Beecham, the local director of a London shipbroking firm, for only £40,000. It was then re-opened to air traffic in September 1955 when Skyways commenced their Continental express coach/air ferry service to Beauvais.

In reality, the general approach by the Ministry to the airfield had been somewhat confused right from the outset. They had once stated that the reason for their indecision as to its ownership came about because the site was not considered part of the integral pattern of UK airports, and therefore subject to constant changes of official policy. The fact remained that if Silver City were to effectively continue their ferrying activities from the Kent coast they would have to find a suitable alternative.

Silver City had initially considered that 400 acres in the St Mary in the Marsh area would be suitable for two 150 ft wide concrete runways of about 4,000 and 4,500 feet in length forming a 'V' and converging near Hope-All-Saints church (the same site as the advanced landing ground of New Romney used by the RAF during the Second World War) but, after the Kent National Farmers Union had objected to this proposal mainly on the basis of 'the disastrous consequences if such an intrusion into some of the finest land in the country was permitted', the quote was revised to a mere 83½ acres.

It was stated at the subsequent council hearing that the original figure of 400 acres had arisen from the fact that six or eight local landowners were involved in the purchase of the necessary 28½ acres of land needed in addition to marsh land. The disclosure of only 83½ acres being required for the projected site must have had the desired effect, for the New Romney Chamber of Commerce were soon fully supporting the application. Although many were still opposed to the idea, eight of the Romney Marsh rural councillors approved the plan in principle, six did not, and three declined to vote. It is interesting to note that the Chairman, who had not voted in two years, felt it necessary to favour the resolution.

Knowing that the acreage available at St Mary in the Marsh could not possibly support their envisaged airport, Silver City then looked into the possibilities of putting down two 200 ft wide runways of about 4,200 and 5,000 feet in length across the Littlestone golf course on The Warren (the same site as the School of Aerial Gunnery at Littlestone during the First World War), but after strong opposition the New Romney Council concluded that although they would be willing to consider any other suitable site within the borough they were not prepared to support this new idea.

August 1953 saw, at last, Lydd Town Council unanimously agreeing to an outline plan for Silver City to build an airfield with buildings in the vicinity of Lydd. After the previous opposition to the other selected sites by farmers who suggested that the nearby beach was good enough to land any aeroplane on, things were to take on a new dimension. In fact, their words were to be taken almost literally.

It was decided that the new airfield could be constructed on Denge Marsh one mile east of the town, part on beach and part on soil, inside the loop of the dismantled railway line near the water tower. The land here, of over 100 acres, was part of 1000 acres that had been bought by the Mayor, Alderman G T Paine, a principal farmer in the area and one who had appreciated the plight of Silver City and foreseen the usefulness of the area as an airport. The site consisted generally of flat meadows and agricultural land, overlying a thin layer of clay with sand and gravels beneath, but interspersed with shingle ridges which were the remains of beaches left by the shifting coastline. Therefore, after three months of searches, Silver City had found a site which not only provided unobstructed approaches and had fairly good road and rail access, but met with all their other requirements.

The site also provided space for later expansion and development, which was just as well for when preliminary plans were finalised on 4 October 1953 the scheme comprised a 246 acre all-weather airport with two 120 ft wide concrete runways, of 4,050 and 3,500 feet effective operational lengths laid in the conventional 'X' form. Along with the latest flying and navigational aids there was to be 30,000 sq ft of administration and terminal buildings, car parks, workshops, a service station, licensed bar and restaurant. It was also intended to build a motel, scheduled to open in the spring of 1955, and eventually erect a number of hangars for part of the aircraft maintenance section to be transferred from Blackbushe, the company's existing overhaul base.

The civil engineering contractor Richard Costain Ltd was appointed as both the designers and constructors, full planning approval was given on 5 November and final drawing sets were approved on 14 December 1953. The Silver City director responsible for supervising the contract was General Sir Edwin Morris, KCB, OBE.

Before any works could begin a bridge over the Denge Marsh Sewer had to be built, as well as a 18 ft wide, 1¼-mile long private access road from the local highway to allow the contractors to get their equipment and materials to the site. Whilst this was in hand the surveyors carried out an extensive site survey and laboratory investigations to ascertain the best soil stabilisation method to adopt for the construction of the runways, bearing in mind the difficulties presented by the low-lying ground and a high water table. When the soil investigations were started, and the surveyors took out the first spadefuls of gravel for analysis, they were reminded by Mayor Paine's legal people that they had only been given permission to build on the surface of the ground, and that any deeper excavations should be considered as extraction of gravels for which a licence was necessary. With this in mind investigations were duly completed and it was found that all the materials required for the project, excepting cement and bituminous products, could be found within the perimeter of the site delinated for the airfield.

Nevertheless, whilst this sub-gravel could be used it was most deficient in fine material and some quantities also contained excessive clays, but an adequate supply of clean gravel was found which contained sufficient sands suitable for stabilising with cement. This was used to form the pavement by spreading a nine-inch layer before compaction, then adding 7%

cement, the latter being incorporated by a single-pass stabiliser to give a finished thickness of six inches. When the paving was set it was surfaced with a wearing coat of tarmacadam, but in areas where abrasive action by aircraft tyres was likely to be excessive the stabilised pavement was covered with 1½ inches of tarred stone, the main landing and take-off areas being sprayed with two layers of tar and gritted with fine sand and stone.

Where the runway cut through shingle ridges the six-inch stabilised gravel pavement was laid directly onto the shingle sub-strata, but where it was underlaid by clays a gravel layer not less than 27 inches thick was interposed between the pavement and the clay. In total about 250,000 cubic yards of clay and other materials were excavated, with the work on the runways being carried out in such a way that the actual bearing stresses that could be applied were about three times as high as those for which it was designed.

One interesting point was that while the gravel and shingle was acceptable, for the reasons given above, it was of such a peculiar nature that it became unstable when compacted by conventional rolling methods. It was desirable to compact the sub-base very densely and therefore minimise the paving thickness, while still achieving a reasonably high load-bearing characteristic, and in order to achieve this a newly-developed compaction method was used which involved high powered vibrating sledges of 1½ to 2 tons, and it was this technology that made the project economically feasible.

As to drainage, it was deemed unnecessary to construct a special system on the site, but where existing ditches crossed any of the works they were diverted through concrete pipes. The only new drainage was a number of vertical drains positioned to pass water through the clay layer in places where there was a risk of localised surface flooding.

With work on the runways (eventually to have effective lengths of 3,300 and 3,595 feet) well under way, construction of the terminal buildings which started in March 1954 was also taking shape. Being predominently of a lightweight steel construction clad in white concrete these structures constituted the first ever airport complex in this country designed especially to handle both vehicles and passengers simultaneously. For this reason the layout consisted of three main areas, each completely separated by covered 'inward' and 'outward' roadways through which the various vehicles passed on arrival and for departure.

Except for the two-storey central section, which housed the radio and control systems, the 300 ft long by 100 ft deep building was generally single storey with a 10'-0" ceiling height throughout. The layout was such that Customs and Immigration offices adjoined the traffic roadways whilst the passenger handling sections, baggage operatives and freight handling areas were separated by the two-storey centre section.

The passenger and reception lounges were finished in modern decor and, in addition to the traffic counters, contained AA and RAC offices, a branch of Lloyds Bank and a small shop. Next to the reception hall was a snack bar, licenced bar and restaurant served by an electric kitchen. The restaurant, capable of seating 100 people, was separated from the tarmac by a glass wall, beyond which was an open air restaurant and the public enclosure. In the most northern section was a bonded store and freight transit sheds, as well as operations and crew briefing rooms, meteorological section, staff dining room and a number of other sections.

To ensure adequate parking for six Bristol Freighter aircraft the tarmac area, which faced the terminal buildings, was located within the western apex formed by the intersection of the two runways. Permanent tie-down points were sunk into the the concrete so as to minimise the possibility of an aircraft overturning in the strong winds the exposed location was subject to. Three taxi strips led to the runway, and were so positioned as to be within a few yards of an aircraft's landing run.

For maximum efficiency Flying Control was linked by Creed teleprinter direct to the Ministry of Transport, as well as the Civil Aviation Authority's master flying control unit at Uxbridge. Other teleprinters linked the airport with Lympne and the company's London headquarters.

The natural gravels strata at Lydd can be seen in this shot of earthmoving plant working on the northern end of runway 14. The new terminal is underway behind (SCA photo).

On the first day of services at Ferryfield (Lydd) on 14 July 1954 passengers for Le Touquet leave the new terminal to board SCA Freighter Mk 21 G-AIME, 'City of Exeter' (hands up the only man not wearing a shirt and tie!) (SCA photo).

Taken on 3 October 1954 and showing the transit car park at Lympne for cars destined for import or export, in the latter case left-hand drive Hillman Minxes. The 'temporary' wartime nature of the airfield buildings is again apparent (SCA photo).

Dark clouds roll over Lympne on 3 October 1954 when all SCA Lympne services moved over to Ferryfield. Freighter Mk 32 G-AMWD 'City of Leicester' is in front of the 'Lydd' arrivals marquee with the corner of the 'Lydd' reception hall marquee on the right. Air Kruise retained their maintenance and other facilities on site after Silver City had left (SCA photo).

Staff at Lympne in front of SCA Freighter Mk 21 G-AGVC 'City of Sheffield' on the last day of services. G-AIME is in the left background with its crew escape hatch open while under the port wing of 'GVC can just be seen the airfield control tower. Mr E Manley Walker, the operations manager, is beneath the port nose door with folded arms (SCA photo).

Mr E Manley Walker outside the Meteorological Office after taking the Silver City Airways flag at Lympne down for the last time on 3 October 1954 (SCA photo).

For communications a Decca 424 airfield control radar was installed, which enabled the location and identification of aircraft up to 16 miles away. A similar aid was installed at Le Touquet which gave flying controllers at both terminals the ability to track aircraft over the greater part of the cross-channel routes. Other aids comprised a m/f directional beacon (flashing the call sign 'FL' in green Morse every 12 seconds), as well as three VHF radio transmitters and receivers, which provided for continuous communications between the airport flying control and aircraft.

For aircraft towing, general tarmac liason and fire control several new Douglas Tugmaster four-wheel drive vehicles, each capable of moving more than 25 tons, were utilised whilst for emergencies a fully-equipped fire engine and ambulance were available. All these were in direct radio contact with the control tower. Aircraft refuelling was carried out by 500-gallon Thomson vehicles, working in pairs to save time, which were fed from three 10,000 gallon surface tanks located near to the service station on the airport access road.

Night flying was catered for by the approach to the main runway being marked by sodium light funnels, which in turn led to portable runway edge lighting (designed by Silver City) placed at 60 yd intervals along each side of the runway.

By July 1954, with all the preparatory work completed 'Ferryfield', as the airport was now officially known, was formally handed over to its operating company, Ferry Airports Ltd, a company formed for the purpose by Britavia Ltd, Silver City's parent company. It had been intended that Silver City continue operations purely in charter and ferrying, which was more desirable than having them act also as airport managers, particularly as this was an area in which their only previous involvement had been through their parent company's undertakings for other clients. Silver City would therefore pay rental and landing fees in the normal way to Ferry Airports, who then sub-contracted the business of operating the restaurant to Graham Lyons (Motels) Ltd who already ran the Royal Oak Motel near to Lympne Airport, at Newingreen, and had plans to open Ferryfields proposed new motel.

Therefore in just under seven months, at an approximate cost of £300,000, Silver City had opened the first international civil airport built in this country since London Airport ten years previous at ten times the cost.

Sub-contractors on the project were:-

Cellulin Flooring Co Ltd	Passenger hall and buffet
City Display Organisation	interior decor
William E Farrer Ltd	sewage disposal plant
Folkestone Waterworks Co	mains water supply
G N Haden & Sons Ltd	heating (boiler house and central heating)
E A Hetherington Ltd	glazing (doors, windows and screens)
K Hills	plumbing (internal and external)
Kent Fencing Co Ltd	boundary fences
F McNeill & Co Ltd	roofs
S J Middleton & Co Ltd	Artex decorative ceilings
Millers Machinery Co Ltd	well point equipment
W Moon	cattle-proof fencing
F Oldham	painting and decorating
Sommerfields Ltd	structural steelwork
South Eastern Electricity Board	mains electric supply
Val de Travers Asphalte Paving Co Ltd	service station roof
Williams & Williams Ltd	metal windows and doors.

Ground equipment suppliers were:-

Decca Radar Ltd	Radar aids
Derby Aviation Ltd	refuellers

Douglas Equipment Ltd	towing vehicles
Hythe Engineering Co Ltd	vehicle loading ramps and accessories
Walter Kidde & Co Ltd	specialist on-vehicle fire fighting equipment
Lamson Paragon Supply Co Ltd	tubes
Martin Walter & Co	Bedford utilities
R W Munroe Ltd	meteorological equipment
Nu-Way Matting Co	ramp matting
Pye (Radio) Ltd	towing vehicle radios
Pyrene Co Ltd	specialist on-vehicle fire fighting equipment
Racal Ltd	communications advisers
Shell-Mex & BP Ltd	fuel and oils.

Silver City Airways – 1954 (the end of Lympne)

Silver City had originally planned that Ferryfield (Lydd) would be finished by Easter 1954 and they would commence operations from there on 1 June with a service to Le Touquet, to replace that previously flown from Lympne, but due to bad weather conditions during the winter months the contractors had not been able to get the runways finished on time (despite what Messrs Costain proclaimed in their house magazine). Therefore in order to cater for the Lydd traffic the Base Manager at Lympne, Mr E Manley Walker, who was supposedly a dab hand at organising such things, set up a second terminal complex near to the existing one. Being completely separate from all other operations there this temporary terminal sited behind the hangars consisted of a marquee together with its own car park, vestibule, check-in, reception, crew rooms and the other necessary facilities. Frantic letters to passengers stressed that as Lydd was not yet ready they should proceed to Lympne as before, whereupon on entering the airport all traffic was directed to either continue to the normal reception areas for Lympne flights, or turn towards the 'Lympne (Lydd)' area for the new services. In effect the airfield and tarmac was split into two in order to deal with Lydd services until the new airfield was ready.

This tented 'circus' worked extremely well, but during the short time the marquees (rented from Black & Edgingtons) were in use one small point had been overlooked. As the ground level was slightly uneven, but had been cut to cricket-pitch length grass beforehand, those areas inside the tent were overlaid with coconut matting. After a few weeks the staff subtly enquired who mowed the airfield grass, and suggested that the groundsman might like to do inside the marquee as well for, due to the damp conditions which prevailed in the early mornings, the grass had grown to a depth of 2" over the top of the matting. Following this request, and to the amusement of all, the lawnmower was lifted in through the side flaps and ran around between the counters and furniture to cut the grass inside.

Mike de Woolfson, one of the counter staff at Lympne during this period, and later to be the Commandant at Lydd Airport, recalled that pilots enjoyed attempting to blow the marquees over either at magneto test or by 'jazzing' the throttles on taxying out of the parking area.

Nevertheless evidence of Ferryfield's completion was apparent on 22 June when, two days after the contractors were asked if the runways were ready, one of Silver City's Freighters made six or seven passes over the airfield and landed twice before returning to Lympne. There was further activity at the airport on 30 June when Air Commodore Powell arrived with a press contingent in his own (but registered to Silver City) twin-engined de Havilland Dragonfly, G-AEWZ, to witness taxying trials carried out by G-ANWG, the first of the company's Mk 32 Freighters to land there, only six days after its delivery from Filton. On this occasion the crew were Captains L Madelaine and D Flett, the same crew that flew the first Silver City Mk 32, G-AMWA, into Lympne on 31 March 1953. At this initiation it was explained that while Lympne could still be used for the existing Ostende and proposed Calais services only the Le Touquet service would be operated from Ferryfield. It was also pointed out, however, that the activity capacity of Ferryfield would ultimately depend on the decision by the MTCA regarding the future of Lympne, which even by this time was not known.

Silver City Airways - 1954

Whilst the company's thoughts early in 1954 were generally occupied with the building of Ferryfield, the spring was to see some unusual events at Lympne. During April a special car badge was introduced so that passengers could commemorate travelling on the services, whilst in May a Mr Nuttall flew with his penny farthing bicycle to Le Touquet. This latter occasion celebrated the first ever crossing of the English Channel 80 years previous when an English cyclist travelled to Dieppe for a Continental holiday and gave the French their first sight of such a machine. Mr Nuttall had initially cycled the nine miles from Ashford to Lympne then, after arrival at Le Touquet, continued 40 miles to the site of the battle of Agincourt before returning home.

Silver City were also going ahead with plans to start a new vehicle ferry service between Lympne and Calais, which had been agreed in Autumn 1953. Inaugurated on 1 June it was approved for operation up to 11 October 1961 but had only been made possible due to the newly completed Calais-Marck Airport which had all its facilities designed and constructed specifically to meet the demands of the vehicle ferry industry in much the same way as the municipality of Le Touquet had done in developing their Paris-Plage Airport at a cost of some £500,000. Planned and financed by the Calais Chamber of Commerce the terminal was built in an incredible 42 days on the site of the Second World War aerodrome and came into use on 1 May. When finished the two runways of 3,600 and 2,950 feet in length were in compacted earth, although they were to be replaced by concrete that Autumn when concrete taxiways, a tarmac apron and hangars were also provided (in 1959 - the same year that Madame Bleriot opened the new terminal building, the 'Aerogare Bleriot' - the longer runway was increased in length to 4,100 ft, by 120 ft wide). Typical single rates for the service would be £6-1s-6d for a Morris, £10-16s for a Vanguard and £15-6s for a Rolls Royce. Motorcycles were £1-7s up to 250cc, £2-0s-6d for those over 250cc, and bicycles 4/6d.

The daily 90-minute return operation by Silver City between Birmingham (Elmdon) and Le Touquet was finally inaugurated on 17 June, after a scheduled vehicle ferry service between May and October had been approved by the M.C.A. for each year up to 31 October 1961, but very soon was to hit snags. Only 370 vehicles had been uplifted when Silver City made the announcement that the service would be suspended indefinitely, not due to a shortfall in bookings but because of 'a general shortage of aircraft' brought about by 'unserviceability and ground incidents' at Elmdon.

Initially the service had been planned to run experimentally until 9 September and then, if successful, yearly between May and October but when in December Mr Eon C Mekie, the

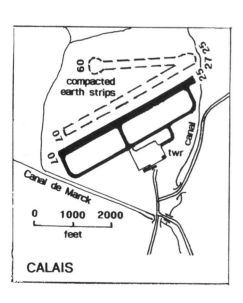

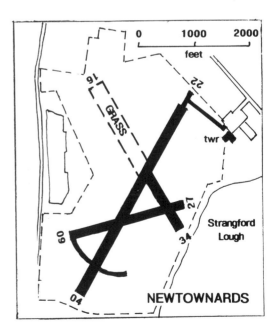

chairman of both Britavia Limited and Silver City, gave a press conference regarding Silver City's activities during 1955 he stated that the reason the company had cancelled this route was because a considerable amount of money had been lost in maintaining it between June and August. Single rates for the service were:- £18 for cars up to 12'-6" and £20 up to 13'-6", £2-5s for motorcycles over 250cc, bicycles 2/6d, and passengers £2-10s. Off peak fares for the first three categories were £6, £9 and £2 respectively.

Although the initial request for the service had come from the AA, insufficient traffic had resulted to warrant it continuing, and whilst it was thought that another attempt at this service might be made later if more customers were likely, the reality remained that even though the fares were less than four times those for the Silver City route from Ferryfield to Le Touquet, and the distance from Elmdon was four times greater, this did not attract passengers and cars from the Midlands. The service was thus never resumed.

With Ferryfield airport now fully operational, the inaugural flight went out at 0800 on Tuesday, 13 July 1954, carrying the Mayor and Mayoress and other invited members of Lydd Town Council to Le Touquet. The occasion turned out to be a memorable one for all present, the passengers were feted, shown around the complex and finally given presents before boarding. The success of the venture was drunk to in champagne and after the Mayor, Alderman Paine, had wished the enterprise well Mr Eoin C Mekie declared that it was 'the day they had waited a long time for'.

Whilst other speeches and toasts were being made two cars, a motorcycle and a scooter were loaded into the company's newest 'Superfreighter', and with this aircraft waiting on the tarmac to take them to Le Touquet the fifteen passengers, of whom only Alderman Paine and his wife were from Kent, took their seats for the inaugural flight. On arrival at the French terminal the guests were shown around the newly modified airport complex and toured the town before returning to Ferryfield later that afternoon.

At the time of the inaugural flight from Ferryfield the new airport was also visited by a contingent of VIPs. Amongst these were Sir Donald Anderson, the deputy chairman and managing director of the Peninsular and Orient Steam Navigation Company, Sir William Currie, chairman of P & O, and Mr Ian Cooper, chairman and managing director of the General Steam and Navigation Company. The reason for the predominence of P & O 'top brass' was that in February 1954 the Britavia group of companies had, through the General Steam and Navigation Company, been taken over by the P & O group. This amalgamation was further complemented on 1 May when Air Kruise (Kent) Ltd became a subsidiary of Britavia Ltd, and subsequently moved to Ferryfield when Lympne closed in October 1954. Air Kruise was formed in August 1946 by Wing Commander Hugh Kennard and pioneered the idea of inclusive tours, a combination of motor coach and air transport with an all-in tariff very similar to the modern day package holiday.

With the cessation of services from Lympne on 13 July all the administration and furniture needed at Ferryfield the following day had to be completely moved before the fare-paying public could be carried that same day. Each item was numbered and palletised and, as soon as the last Freighter returned to Lympne at the end of that day's services, it was loaded with as much as possible and flown with two vehicle loaders to Ferryfield to be off-loaded. In 1½ hours everything was unloaded but took the rest of the night to be installed in its required place, the operation to move one airport to another going on into the small hours and being carried out amongst electricians and painters putting the finishing touches in. By early morning, when the new set-up was complete, staff were sent away for a few hours sleep before starting work proper at 0600. After the frantic activity of the night before all went smoothly on this first day, when 68 services were recorded, and the public had no idea of what had gone on behind the scenes in order to get everything ready for them.

In August Silver City was chartered to carry a single engine bearing measuring 8'-3" in diameter, which needed a special carriage frame to get it into the Freighter, but much of this latter half of the year was more notable for its applications for service approvals.

During August the Ministry gave, subject of course to their usual provisos, approval for Silver City to operate a ten-year, cross-Channel helicopter service alongside their existing vehicle ferry routes, but specifically between Lympne or Lydd and Calais, Ostende and Le Touquet. When it became available Boulogne was to be included, with a possible frequency of more than 100 flights envisaged using either the Westland/Sikorsky S51 or Bristol 171 types, both on separate services but only in direct support of the vehicle ferry operations as no helicopters were available to the company at that time that could carry the amount of payload necessary to make a cross-Channel service of this type a viable proposition.

The company's venture into helicopters had started back in 1952 but it was not until July 1953 that they actually operated one. A Westland/Sikorsky S51, G-ANAL, owned by the Evening News, was flown and maintained by Silver City from their Blackbushe base, and two months later was the first civilian helicopter to land on Guernsey. In 1952 they had expressed an interest in the possible use of large, twin-engined helicopters carrying cars or freight in detachable panniers. Carrying a similar load to a Freighter, two cars and up to twelve passengers seated in an observation saloon at the front end of the unit, a helicopter could release the outgoing pannier and pick up the ingoing one in a matter of moments, in terms of turnround time.

On 17 August Silver City's own Westland/Sikorsky S51, G-ANLV, was seen for the first time in the company livery at London's South Bank heliport. They had initially proposed to operate the type in the carriage of spare car parts and general freight for the coming eight months, the intention being then to commence an air freight service between Lydd and Le Touquet on 1 April 1955.

As with many of the company's progressive ideas, use of the then available helicopters for transportation of freight or passengers was not really economically feasible in the United Kingdom, which was not yet conditioned for the introduction of such services. The idea of allowing wingless aircraft to fly over, and land within the centres of, cities or towns without there being adequate unobstructed approaches and clear surrounding areas was quite unthinkable – only in some foreign cities could one witness such luxuries. This did not, however, prevent Mr Mekie from operating a helicopter into the grounds of his house at Woodmansterne, Surrey in July 1955, after attending a cocktail party at the RAC Club, Epsom to mark the 40th anniversary of Westland Aircraft Ltd.

Eventually the only mention of such helicopter services was in June 1955 when, in a House of Commons debate, the Minister of Transport, Mr J A Boyd-Carpenter, told of a scheme in which the Port of London Authority and London County Council had been approached as to the possibility of building a landing platform to replace that of the South Bank Station. He also spoke of eight local authorities who had mentioned specifically their interest in an inter-city helicopter service, and of some 80 local authorities who had sought advice about the reservation of suitable sites for future air stations. Nevertheless although these talks, and the ideas discussed, were the foundations upon which all British passenger helicopter services were to be based, (and indeed a number of British airlines did later take up the idea) Silver City's proposals for using vehicle-ferrying helicopters were far too progressive for the time and the idea was eventually dropped.

Silver City Airways – 1955

In October 1954 the company had applied to the ATAC for vehicle ferry rights to run a seasonal summer service between Lydd and/or Southampton to Le Havre and/or Deauville, the first of which materialised on 6 April 1955 when the 50 minute inaugural flight went out from Southampton to St Gatien Airport, Deauville. This 127-mile route had approval from the MTCA to operate up to 31 December 1961 but was not given as much publicity as some of the company's other services, even though it was at the time the longest air ferry service to the Continent. On 21 May this route was chosen to celebrate the 50,000th 'in service' crossing of the English Channel by the company when their Freighter Mk 32, G-ANWI, carried a party headed by Mr Mekie and was greeted at Deauville by the town mayor, M Fossorier. Among the other passengers on board were a Mr & Mrs B Campbell of the Great Yarmouth boat building firm, who also wrote a slice of history by taking with them their Bentley towing an Albatross speedboat on its trailer.

As to the service itself, which started initially as a single daily flight in each direction but increased to two flights per day during the summer season between 25 May and 3 October, it left Southampton at 1130 and 1430 and Deauville at 1300 and 1600 hrs. During the high season cars were charged from £30 return and passengers £10, whilst a single fare applied for motorcycles up to 250cc of £3, and larger machines of £4-10s, with combinations and three-wheelers being charged £6. Autocycles and scooters were £2 single, with motorised cycles and accompanying passengers 5s. During the off-peak period the fares for all solos, autocycles and scooters were reduced by 10s, and combinations by £1, but in all the latter cases the return fare was double the single rate.

With regard to the Southampton to Le Havre route, Silver City had originally envisaged a freight and passenger service running between these two towns as the British Transport Commission intended to close their own sea ferry service on this route. However, after objections to the BTC proposal by 30 factions caused a subsequent enquiry Silver City, who had hoped to start their service in November 1955, decided to delay the scheme so as not to prejudice the case at the enquiry.

Nevertheless, while these discussions were going on there were many who had considered that this projected service was a general part of Silver City's philosophy of increasing their cross-Channel ferry services in the coming year, but in February 1956 the BTC agreed to retain their steamer services and Silver City abandoned the idea, pointing out that they had only intended to use Dakotas on the service and not the Bristol Freighter.

In 1954 Britavia Ltd, which hitherto had merely been the holding company for the group, became operational when they acquired a fleet of Hermes aircraft generally for use in the transportation of troops but for other long-range charters as well. Consequently, on 1 April 1955, the holding company name was changed to British Aviation Services Limited while the existing BAS operations were carried on in Britavia's name.

In December 1954 Silver City had again applied to the ATAC, this time for a license to run a vehicle ferry service between West Freugh (Stranraer) and Newtownards (Belfast) as well as an all-freight service between Blackbushe and Newtownards to call in at Birmingham and Woodvale, Liverpool. A separate application was also recorded for routes between Elmdon, Blackbushe, Formby and Belfast.

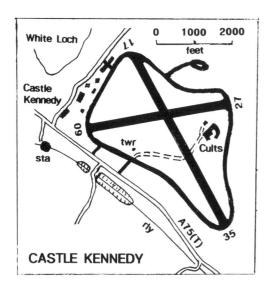

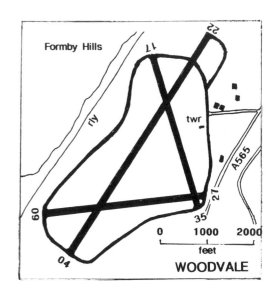

The first of these services was inaugurated on Tuesday, 7 April 1955, not between West Freugh as planned but from Castle Kennedy airfield, situated 3½ miles east of Stranraer, to Newtownards (known locally as 'Ards' and owned by Messrs Short Brothers and Harland) in County Down, ten miles east of Belfast. The route proving flight had been undertaken 14 days previous on 24 March by one of the company's Freighters Mk 32, G-ANWF, piloted by Captain A Cussons and Flight Officer F Russell, and was a route Air Commodore Powell had, in the Belfast News Letter of February 1953, expressed a desire to open a service on. For its first working cargo into Ards 'NWF carried a party of officials and two Nuffield Organisation cars which had only come off the assembly line the previous Wednesday, one being a Morris Oxford for delivery to the Belfast company of W H Alexander Ltd, and the other a MG Magnette for Messrs Leslie Porter Ltd.

When the aircraft arrived at Newtownards its ten passengers, who included Air Commodore Powell and Mr S A Tennant, joint managing directors of Ferry Airports Ltd, were met by Mr R J Fizzell, manager of the Northern Ireland Tourist Board, Mr I Williams of the Ulster Tourist Development Association, a party of travel agents and press representatives. There then followed a press conference at which it was stated that the company had first intended to use West Freugh in Wigtownshire as their terminal but after some difficulties had changed to Castle Kennedy when it was realised that the latter, a disused wartime field on the Earl of Stair's Lochinch estate, was more readily usable. However, and more to the point, they had placed themselves in direct competition with British Railway ferry ships that operated between Stranraer and Larne. Also, considering that the new 35-mile service including loading preliminaries would only take 35 minutes, with a flight time of just 18 minutes as against 8½ hours by sea, a distinct possibility existed for an intense competition to develop between sea and air ferries, even though the established British Railway boats were in a stronger position.

Indeed, and possibly due to Silver City's plans, between June and September 1955 British Railways transferred to the Stranraer service the 'Hampton Ferry', a Dover train ferry vessel which was known to have carried up to 100 cars and 800 passengers, the idea being to supplement the existing ferry ships which comprised 'The Princess Margaret', capable of carrying up to 16 cars and 1,400 passengers, and 'The Princess Maud', which was slightly larger and capable of taking on a few more cars but only occasionally put into service.

When the official inauguration flight was undertaken in April, after the service had been duly approved by the ATAC for operation up to 31 December 1961, the route was then formally opened by Mr J Henderson Stewart MP, Under Secretary of State for Scotland, in the presence of directors and officials of the company, representatives of Wigtown County and Stranraer Town Councils, amongst others. To give an indication of some of the 90 or so guests who attended the formalities, these included the Earl of Stair, Lord Lieutenant of Wigtownshire and Lady Stair, Lord Inchcape, Sir Donald F Anderson, Sir Patrick Dollan, chairman of the Scottish Advisory Council for Civil Aviation, Sir Edwin Morris, Mr Ian M Hooper, Mr L D Gumley, member of the Scottish Advisory Council for Civil Aviation, Colonel R A Armstrong, chairman of the Dumfries and Galloway Devopment Association, Air Vice Marshal S D Macdonald, general manager of Britavia Ltd, and members of Silver City's directorship including Air Commodore Powell, Mr Mekie and Mr S A Tennant.

Soon after the formal opening had taken place the company's Freighter Mk 21, G-AGVC, took off amidst falling rain for Newtownards with a number of official passengers and two more cars - a Morris Cowley saloon and a Morris Minor. Among the others who made the trip were Provost A A Walker of Stranraer and town clerk Mr R McInnes Wilson, Mr S A Berry (Chief Constable of Dumfries and Galloway), Mr D A Aitken, the county clerk of Wigtownshire, and Mr J H Mackie, the MP for Galloway. Previous to this one of Silver City's Dakotas had arrived before the ceremony with the London contingent and had also left for Newtownards. On arrival both parties were met at the airport by the Mayor, Alderman Isaac Baxter, and taken to the town hall, before attending a lunch at the Grand Hotel in Belfast where Lord Glentoren, the Minister of Commerce in Northern Ireland, and Mr Henderson Stewart were the principal guests. Afterwards, due to foggy conditions at

Stranraer, the party from there were unable to make the return trip on Thursday afternoon and had to wait in Belfast until the fog lifted on the Friday morning.

With regard to the operation, three daily services were initially scheduled to run in each direction, timed to leave Newtownards at 1030, 1300 and 1530 hrs, and returning from Castle Kennedy at 1110, 1340 and 1610 hrs, but on Wednesdays the first flights from each terminal did not run. Single rates for the service were £7 for cars up to 12'-6" in length and £10 up to 14'-0", then a rate of £2-10s per foot applied up to 17'-6" after which cars were charged £17-10s. Motorcycles under 250cc were £1-10s, over 250cc £2-5s, sidecars £3, autocycles and scooters £1, and bicycles (whether powered or not) 2/6d each way. The return fare for passengers was £5.

As for the all-freight Blackbushe to Newtownards route things were not to be so easy. It had been Silver City's intention to start this service on Tuesday, 5 April, two days before the start of the Stranraer to Newtownards service, but after constant requests for a vehicle ferry service between Woodvale and Ireland had come to nothing, the company then revised the application for a vehicle ferry service between Woodvale and Newtownards. At this time the idea was to operate the vehicle ferry and freight services together, but by the beginning of April when the company had only received preliminary approval to run solely a vehicle ferry service up to 31 December 1961, due to interpretation of conditions of the licence which forbade the carrying of passengers with freight, they were forced to amend their plans.

Originally the company had not intended to operate a vehicle ferry from the Liverpool area until 1956 as it was felt that the fares would seem high when compared with those charged on their optimum routes from Lydd to Le Touquet and Calais, and between Stranraer and Belfast. Therefore on 17 June, the same day as the Birmingham to Le Touquet service was inaugurated, when the 127-mile, 60 minute Woodvale to Newtownards route was officially opened by the company's Freighter Mk 21, G-AGVC, Silver City had decided to restrict the operation to an on-demand only daily return service.

Whilst the first scheduled flight carried the three crew and seven passengers, including Mr E Manley-Walker, and Messrs D J McKeirnan and W C Hosegood of the AA and RAC respectively, along with two cars from a Liverpool car agency for delivery to Belfast, the service was destined to be short-lived. In fact other than at the beginning of April, when one of the Mk 32s carried out a proving flight between Blackbushe and Newtownards with a consignment of Britannia components for the second production line at the Belfast works of Messrs Short Brothers and Harland, the company only carried out the occasional service between the vehicle ferry terminals during 1955. The result of this was that, in December, the Southport Guardian reported that 'the air ferry service started during the summer had been temporarily suspended due to a general shortage of aircraft'.

Although the service was never reintroduced, whilst it was in operation the rates for cars were £20-10s up to 12'-6", rising to £33-15s for those over 15'-6", motor-cycles under 250cc were charged £4-10s and those over £6, combinations and three-wheelers £8, autocycles and scooters £2-5s, and bicycles 5s. Passengers could be carried, but only when they were accompanying a vehicle, the fare being £3-14s single and £7-8s return.

While all these latter mentioned services were only instigated during 1954, the company's actual operation during that year resulted in their aircraft having made 20,870 flights and carrying over 126,000 passengers. Of these, 112,214 passengers and 42,507 vehicles were carried solely on the vehicle ferry side on 18,210 flights, during the course of which the Freighters each averaged 2,662 landings. History was also made on 27 July when their aircraft crossed the Channel no fewer than 222 times, this being one of the most intensive operations in the history of world air transport up to that time.

With regard to the company's Ferryfield operations, when the last Le Touquet service from Lympne went on Sunday 3 October 1954, using Freighter G-AGVC, the Calais and Ostende services which had been suspended during the winter months were reinstated in the coming spring at the new airport. This elevated the total amount of traffic handled through Lydd during the first year of operation up to 13 July 1955 to 88,621 passengers and 54,032 vehicles, a figure also helped by the activities of Air Kruise who had moved to Lydd when Lympne closed. In August alone, Ferryfield handled nearly twice as much cargo than any other British airport, a total of 6,680 tons, Lympne being second with 3,802 tons.

1955 had opened with the Southampton to Deauville, Stranraer to Newtownards, and the belated Woodvale to Newtownards services but there was also a report of another projected service. After a meeting of the Council of Galloway Chamber of Commerce, at which they decided to write to Silver City at Belfast asking if they could initiate a vehicle ferry service between the twenty-six counties and England, the end of April saw an article in the Irish Times stating that Silver City had completed the necessary preliminary plans for operating such a service into Dublin.

In actual fact, although there was much speculation at the time, such a service had first to be cleared under the provisions of the Anglo-Irish Air Agreement of 1946 whereby BEA's associate, Aer Lingus, had a complete monopoly in the choice of scheduled and unscheduled air traffic between Britain and Ireland. As things were to turn out, a lot of water was to pass under the bridge before such a service was to be undertaken.

There was another interesting flight between Lydd and Calais on Tuesday, 28 July when M. Jean Salis, a 59-year old French airman, flew a replica of Louis Bleriot's 1909 monoplane between Calais and Ferryfield. On 25 July 1909 Bleriot had made the first cross-Channel flight between Calais and Dover, in a flimsy machine built of wood and fabric and powered by a 3-cylinder, 22-hp Anzani engine, thus winning for himself the £1,000 prize offered by a British newspaper. On arrival Bleriot crashlanded in a meadow behind Dover's ancient Norman castle, the aircraft later being covered by a marquee and people charged a fee to see it, with the resulting proceeds going to charity. Bleriot died in 1936 at the age of 64.

For the re-enactment of this historic flight, which was only achieved after four days of hesitancy due to the weather conditions prevailing on both sides of the Channel, M. Salis used an aircraft he had made himself in his own workshops near Paris with the original intention of using it in the making of a film on Bleriot's life that never materialised.

On taking off from Calais on the evening of the 28th, and being escorted by a number of other aircraft (including 2 Austers of the Southend Flying School, piloted by B Warman & G Tame), M. Salis crossed the English coastline five miles west of the field where Bleriot had landed before turning for Ferryfield. On his arrival, elated by his success and to the sound of cheering crowds, some thirty people rushed to his aircraft on the runway and hustled him off to a champagne celebration party, whilst his aircraft was hangared before being flown back to Calais the following day in one of Silver City's Freighters.

The following Sunday was to see a similar flight when M. Juan de la Bruyere, a 27-year old Canadian building contractor and grandson of Bleriot, also flew across the Channel in a replica of his grandfather's monoplane. On this occasion, however, de la Bruyere made the return trip from Calais to Dover and did not land in England.

Although there had been more than just a strong rumour that these latter events caused Silver City's operations at Ferryfield to fall into complete chaos through the over-eagerness of the waiting press journalists the company's operation on the whole during 1955 had indeed been an impressive one, the total vehicles carried having increased by 34% and that for the passenger division by 48% over the 1954 figures. On vehicle ferry services they had carried no fewer than 57,101 items made up of 44,670 cars, 8,774 motorcycles and 3,657 bicycles. They had also carried 166,219 passengers in a total of 23,718 individual ferry flights with each of their fifteen Bristol Freighters (six Mk 21 and nine Mk 32), and averaged on all operations 3,414 landings and takeoffs. The company's most productive day was on 2 July when, on all their Continental routes, they carried over 600 vehicles and 1,500 passengers in only 165 trips which constituted a new record load for one day. On this day their Lydd to Le

Touquet service alone moved 1,064 passengers, 235 cars, 157 motorcycles, 35 bicycles and 8,569 lbs of freight. Lydd also handled nearly 20,000 tons of freight in 1955, more than any other British airport to the total of 57,584 tons, whilst London Airport handled 37,974 tons.

During August Silver City became involved with an article known as the 'Legumex', this unusual name being given to a new type of rotary potato peeler made in France by Messrs Moulin Legumes, which was being introduced into the UK by McLellan Associates Ltd, a London-based company. To enable McLellan to distribute a consignment of 2,000 peelers, packed in 500 boxes weighing approximately five tons, as quickly as possible it was decided to hire one of the Freighters, thus on 12 August at 2130 hrs one of the Mk 21s, suitably draped with the appropriate advertisments, arrived at Lydd with the first of these loads.

An unusual charter carried out during August was the transfer of the complete contents of an Amsterdam oil company officials' house to a research centre at Sittingbourne. Members of the family were also included in the successful move, which then prompted a further ten work colleagues and their families to use this 'removal service' in the following weeks. For this exercise the furniture was picked up from Schipol Airport and flown to Lydd, from where it was loaded into a van and driven to the new homes.

With the proposal to eventually develop a new freight service to thirty cities in Belgium, France, Germany, Holland, Scandinavia and Switzerland, 1 November was to see the start of yet another cross-Channel service in the form of the all-freight 'Roadair' lift between Lydd and Calais. Utilising the existing air ferry facilities the service connected with road transport at both terminals and initially operated once a day in each direction, but this frequency was allowed to be increased the following Spring. Rates for the operation were approximately £12-10s per ton of freight up to a maximum of five tons with lower fees applying to some commodities. The media initially termed it a freight 'tramp' service.

Also in October 1954, after having gained experience on its previous Alpine flights, Silver City had made applications to the ATAC to operate a vehicle ferry service between Lydd and Basle. This route was to be seasonal, from mid-December to the end of the Easter holiday each year, and use the unheated Freighter Mk 32 operating in both directions on Fridays, Saturdays and Sundays. It was intended to commence this 400-mile, two hour 40 minute 'winter sports enthusiasts' service on 16 December 1955 and run it until 30 April 1961 but, although the company endeavoured to make a success of the operation, the new Alpine holiday agencies organizing cheap charter flights into Swiss and Austrian resorts at the time prevented the viability of this vehicle ferry service.

This uncertainty did not stop the first of the scheduled flights taking place when the Nuffield Organisation booked all the available freight space in order to ship three urgently-needed MGA cars to their Swiss distributor, Heinz Keller of Zurich. The flight was undertaken by G-ANWG, but had its shortcomings when hampered by the French authorities' insistence that they fly at over 11,000 ft throughout due to heavy cloud and the crew having to find Basle solely by their own navigation due to a strike by French air traffic controllers.

Had the service continued, with the outward flight scheduled to leave Lydd at 0900 and return from Basle at 1500 hrs, the rates would have been comparible with previous flights whereby cars up to 12'-6" in length would have been charged £25, £35 over 12'-6" and £45 for those over 14'-6", with return fares double the single rate. For motorcycles the charge would have been £10 and for combinations £15. Only passengers accompanying their vehicles would have been carried, the fares being £15-3s single and £27-6s return with a 50% reduction for children under 12 years of age.

During the year the company flew 5,205,798 revenue short ton miles and claimed a new freight record by uplifting 72,333 tons of carge in its aircraft, this being equivalent to 58% of all the air freight handled through British airports in the year. This complemented the award they had received for operating at this world intensity in 1954, the Cumberbatch Trophy, the premier British Commonwealth air safety award that was presented by HRH the

Duke of Edinburgh to Air Commodore Powell on 4 November 1955, on behalf of the Guild of Air Pilots and Air Navigators for what the Guild described as 'their magnificent work on the cross Channel air ferries'. The trophy was awarded annually for outstanding contributions to, or achievements in, air transport safety and marked eight years of Silver City operations between 1948 and 1954 involving well over 60,000 cross Channel flights without an accident resulting in injury or loss of life to a passenger. In winning this award the company were the first independant airline to receive the trophy in over fifteen years.

Silver City Airways - 1956

As for 1956, which was to see the discontinuation of the company's Gatwick to Le Touquet service, it was reported in January just how successful the Stranraer to Newtownards car ferry had been. It the first nine months of its operation between 7 April and 31 December 1955 over 2,100 vehicles and 5,500 passengers had been flown between the two terminals, which represented 25% of the total traffic carried between Stranraer and Ireland by both ship and aeroplane in that period. Due to this the intensity of the service, that had been seven return trips per day during the season, was to be increased to 14 return trips daily for the 1956 season, which in effect resulted in a landing and take-off every 15 minutes during the peak operating periods. As a direct result of the services' success the passenger return fare was reduced by 10s to £4-10s, and in February a general fare review on both the cross Channel and Irish Sea air ferries resulted in a reduction in charges for certain types of family and sports cars of between £5-10s and £7. This ruling applied to all Ford, Triumph, Healey, Porsche and Singer cars not more than 12'-9" long, which were accepted at the rate of vehicles up to 12'-6" in length.

With the invisaged increase in the number of Easter and Summer holidaymakers using their services during 1956 the company introduced a system by which repayments for air tickets could be made more appealing. The scheme, which applied to families and individuals whose tickets had a combined value of £20 or more, allowed the traveller to make a deposit of 10% of the fare with an undertaking to pay the balance over a period of between six and 21 months, depending on the total ticket value.

The start of the year also saw the company make a number of applications for further services, typified by February when they applied to the ATAC for permission to operate six additional scheduled return flights between Stranraer and Newtownards, using Dakotas and Bristol Freighters to carry passengers, freight and mail. In March there was a report of an application made to amend the terms of approval of their Lydd to Calais operation, this service having hitherto been operative on a seasonal Easter to October basis each year but was to be operated for the complete year. It coincided with the company's request to be allowed to combine the all-freight 'Roadair' service between Lydd and Calais with that of the Lydd to Calais vehicle ferry service, a decision brought about due to their inability to run both operations separately through lack of aircraft.

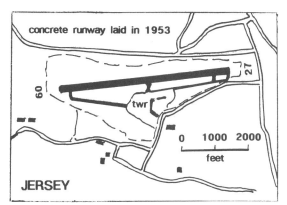
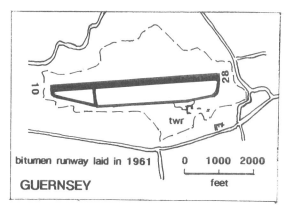

Note the similarities in the layout of these two airports, both with noticeable improvements to the runway by the introduction of asphalt paving in place of the previous grass strips.

Back in July of 1954 Silver City had picked up on one of their previous ideas when they applied for a licence to operate a daily mail, freight and vehicle service between Guernsey and Southampton. Under this application, which ran from 1 October 1954 to 30 September 1961, they were approved to carry up to six passengers per flight, using either Freighter or Dakota aircraft, with supplementary flights as necessary, but it was to be some twenty months before it finally 'took off'.

As the first vehicle ferry service between the British mainland and the Channel Islands, the 120-mile, 45-50 minute schedule was set up principally to deliver perishable food, cars and manufactured goods to the island, and airlift fresh-cut flowers and market garden produce to the mainland. Up to this point in time fresh flowers, particularly, had been sent from Guernsey on the 0900 mail boat to Southampton and on arrival at 1600 were then railed to reach London by 2330, sorted and delivered to Covent Garden. However, by using the air ferry the flowers could be picked much later on in the day, be delivered to London from Southampton by road and still arrive at Covent Garden before midnight. It was estimated that, at the peak of the season, some 30-35% of the total consignment of flowers could be sent by air – this being equivalent to the entire delivery to London.

Finally inaugurated on Monday, 27 February 1956 the flight, carried out by the company's Mk 32, G-AMWB piloted by Captain G Hogarth and co-piloted by Captain C Helliwell, had on board Mr Eon C Mekie CBE, the vice-chairman Mr Ian M Hooper, General Sir Edwin Morris KCB, OBE, MC, and Sir Edward Wilshaw KCMG, directors. Also in the party were Group Captain Deane CBE, assistant to the managing director, Mr E Manly Walker, the air ferries commercial manager, and Mr R McRae, now the Southampton area manager.

On arrival at La Villiaze Airport the aircraft, with its load comprising a Morris Minor car, an autocycle, six bicycles, some tractor oil, whisky, gin, ice cream, cigarettes, fresh meat, tennis rackets, a refrigerator, a kitchen unit and cylinders of medical oxygen, was met by Air Commodore Powell and Mr L R Pavey, his commercial manager, who had arrived the previous day in Powell's Dragonfly. The whole party then attended a civic reception given by the Guernsey States Authorities before they returned home in the same aircraft, which also carried 800 boxes of freshly picked flowers.

Although the 120-mile route was three times longer than Silver City's French air ferries, the rates were only a little higher, a single fare of £12 for cars up to 12'-9" in length, £14-10s up to 13'-6", £17-10s up to 14'-6", £20 up to 15'-6" and for larger cars £23. One item now becoming commonplace on these services was the three-wheeler, which was charged £7-10s, whilst motorcycles were £2-10s up to 250cc and £3-15s over 250cc, combinations were £5 and cycles just 10s. Normally passenger fares were £4-18s single, but from 1 June to 6 October a 15-day excursion return was available at £5-10s on Tuesdays, Wednesdays and Thursdays. Additionally up to 1 March, and from 1 November until 31 December, a special three-day return fare of £4-18s was available to all passengers whose flights had originated in Guernsey. Flowers in cardboard boxes were flown for 1s-2d per box, whilst fresh fruit and frozen vegetables were ferried for just over 2d a pound.

On several occasions previous to this Silver City had come to the rescue of the island's industry, particularly when the meat trade was paralysed by strikes and one which affected all rail transport. On these occasions the island's flower deliveries 'beat the strike' by being flown to their markets, the half a dozen proving flights during 1954 having established the value to Guernsey of Silver City's speedy transport. This was again demonstrated in March 1956 when the Guernsey car distributors, Ruette Braye Motors Ltd, signed an agreement (the first of its kind) to have all their cars and light vans delivered to the island by air.

Also in March there were reports of new developments at Ferryfield (Lydd). With the now ever-increasing demands for both passenger and vehicle ferry services to the Continent the relocation at the airport of Britavia's subsidiary, Air Kruise, had caused a definite strain on the existing terminal facilities, and it was decided to reappoint Richard Costain Ltd to build a completely separate two-storey terminal block solely for Air Kruise passenger services. Of

The entrance to Southend Airport at the end of 1954 showing the Air Charter petrol station with the Customs shed behind it. To the right is the passenger reception hall, while at left is the end of the ATEL 'black' hangar (photo by Highlands Studios, Leigh on Sea, Essex).

The dismantled Sikorsky S-51 helicopter G-AJOR of Autair being loaded into Freighter Mk 31E G-AMSA 'Voyager' of Air Charter Ltd at Southend in the summer of 1956. It was destined for Mestervig, Greenland to be used by a Danish mining company in flying surveyors and equipment around on survey work (photo by Richardsons).

At Ferryfield's official opening on 5 April 1956 the Duke of Edinburgh (at left) watches loading operations from inside SCA Freighter Mk 32 G-AMWD 'City of Leicester' along with (L-R) Air Commodore Powell, Eoin Mekie and Captain C I Hopkins (co-pilot on the flight to Le Touquet with the Duke on board). The pilot, Captain D Flett, is out of sight inside the fuselage (SCA photo).

SCA Freighter Mk 32 G-AMWN at Le Touquet in August 1956 before the name and individual letters were applied (photo by Ken Honey, Gunnislake, Cornwall).

The much-travelled Ford Consul MJN 903 of Doug Whybrow, General Manager for the Channel Air Bridge, being loaded into Freighter Mk 31E G-AMSA "Voyager" from the back of a lorry at Rotterdam on 18 September 1956. It was still two weeks before the airport opened and none of the Freighter loading ramps were on site then (Air Charter photo).

Press and dignitaries surround the flag–bedecked Freighter Mk 32, G–ANVS 'Vigilant' of Channel Air Bridge at the official opening of Rotterdam airport on 1 October 1956, with Tiger Moths from the resident flying school passing over in formation (Dutch Tiger Moths had the longer 'Fokker' fin) (photo by Nationaal Foto Persbureau, Amsterdam).

some 6,600 sq ft this would accommodate the managing director, commercial manager, chief pilot, secretarial and accounts staff on the upper floor, and on the ground floor a reception hall, spacious lounge and self service restaurant, bank, shop, bar and telephone kiosks, along with a traffic office and modern kitchen. In front of the terminal there was to be additional parking for up to 100 cars and it was intended to finish a spectators car park and buffet bar by the coming summer.

With these developments the expansion of Air Kruise since their takeover had been quite prolific. In 1954 they had only carried 16,000 tour passengers between Lympne and Basle, Ostende and Le Touquet, whereas by 1955 the total on their combined coach and air travel services had increased to 47,000 passengers, constituting over ten million passenger flown miles, with additional route to Paris, Dusseldorf and Turin. In just July 1956 the company carried half of their 1955 total, increased its air hostesses from four to nine, and brought in new regular routes to Barcelona, Luxembourg and Palma.

Air Kruise had also intended to increase their fleet of Dakota and Bristol Freighter aircraft acquired since their amalgation from seven to eleven (and subsequently thirteen) by being the first British company to operate the new Handley Page Herald 'branchliner', when it ordered six of the four-Alvis Leonides Major piston-engined aircraft, a decision made at BAS's board meeting on 22 September 1955 and announced by Mr Mekie the same day. The intention was for these aircraft to supplement and eventually replace the older types in company use, but when Handley Page failed to secure this design (the forerunner of the twin-engined Herald) there was talk of buying the Fokker Friendship, one of which landed at Ferryfield in May 1957 for a special visit so that it could be inspected by BAS officials, as a prelude to its display at the Paris Air Show. Soon after this though, Wing Commander Hugh Kennard temporarily disappeared into the sidelines when Air Kruise finally integrated into Silver City on 1 October 1957, and only reappeared when appointed as joint managing director for the latter (he was appointed onto the SCA board on 23/10/56, and resigned on 22/11/60), and even later with his own company, Air Ferry Ltd at Manston.

At the same time as the Air Kruise terminal was being built, additional taxiways to speed up aircraft turnround and a new 27,000 sq ft maintenance hangar for Silver City were also nearing completion. This steel-framed structure at 250 feet long, 122 feet wide and 30 feet high was capable of holding up to three Freighters or Dakotas and able to cope with major overhauls as well as routine periodic maintenance. Along one side of the hangar was sited 3,400 sq ft of single-storey offices, a canteen and stores, the approximate cost of all these developments (including the Air Kruise terminal) being in the region of £200,000.

In the first week of March Silver City's operations at Ferryfield were disrupted for one day when it was found necessary to effect runway repairs, and all services were diverted to Southend Airport. This brief episode was strange in the fact that, in 1954, Air Charter had been refused permission to use Le Touquet as an alternative terminal when Calais airport was temporarily closed, but was by way of a prelude to one of the company's outstanding events of the year when HRH the Duke of Edinburgh visited Ferryfield on 5 April as part of the airports' official opening ceremony (and believed to be the first occasion a member of the Royal Family had visited the Borough of Lydd since a ship carrying George 1 was forced ashore nearby in 1724).

After flying a four-engined de Havilland Heron of the Queens Flight from White Waltham the Duke arrived at the terminal at 1045 and on stepping from the aircraft met Mr Mekie and Air Commodore Powell. After the initial exchanges he was escorted to the main building to be introduced to Mr W G Franklin, Wing Commander Hugh Kennard, Captains L Madelaine and P E Rosser (Silver City's most long-standing pilot, who since Air Kruise's incorporation into the group had been acting as chief pilot for the latter), Mr D Kinnear (airport manager), Mr L Turner (Ferryfield station superintendent) and Mr R MacRae (area superintendent).

On walking through the outward car tunnel beside the control tower the Duke saw vehicles being loaded aboard the next aircraft for Le Touquet before being shown around the tower.

Proceeding by car to the newly completed hangar he then spoke to some very immaculately dressed maintenance staff before entering an Air Kruise Bristol Wayfarer for a closer look at the work being carried out. The Duke was ushered back to the terminal building but declined the use of a car, pausing to watch work being carried out on the new Air Kruise building.

On his return to the main terminal, where a Silver City Freighter Mk 32, G-AMWD, was waiting to take him to Le Touquet for lunch, the Duke visited the traffic office to 'collect his ticket' before being introduced to other officials and guests in the airport restaurant. Among those present was Alderman G T Paine, who that week had been elected Mayor of Lydd for the 25th year.

Ten minutes late, the Duke boarded the aircraft which was loaded with two export cars, a Sunbeam Rapier and a Triumph TR3, and during the 20-minute flight sat alongside Captain D Flett in the co-pilots seat where he took control of the aircraft, the co-pilot Captain C I Hopkins having given up this seat for the flight. Among those on the aircraft were Lieut Michael Parker, the Dukes private secretary, Sqn Ldr Edward Chinnery, the Air Equerry in Waiting, Inspector F Kelly of Scotland Yard, Mr Mekie, Air Commodore Powell, Sir Edwin Morris, Sir Donald Anderson, Sir William Currie and Mr Ian Hooper.

At Le Touquet the party was received by Dr Pouget, president of the local aero club, M G Phalampin, Prefect of the Pas de Calais, and M J H Sainsard the airport manager. After watching the handling of cars and lunching privately the Duke returned to London direct in the Heron that Sqn Ldr B G Stanbridge and Flt Lieut G C Goodyer had flown over from Ferryfield in parallel with the Freighter.

Silver City expanded further in 1956 when BAS announced their controlling interests firstly with Manx Airlines Ltd, then with the Lancashire Aircraft Corporation, and subsequently in 1957 with Dragon Airways Ltd. These three companies were moulded into the northern division of Silver City Airways Ltd with a network of passenger routes covering the Isle of Man, Glasgow, Edinburgh, Leeds, Blackpool, Birmingham, Jersey and certain Continental towns. BAS also acquired Manx Airlines associate company, Manx Aero Engineering Ltd.

The move was first publicly reported in March after four officials from both Silver City and Manx Airlines arrived back in England from discussions at Newtownards Airport. The contingent, who included Mr B Lamplough (air superintendent), Mr B Wallace (traffic superintendant) and Captain L Madelaine from Silver City and Mr Kavanagh of Manx Airlines, then went to Renfrew and Newcastle-on-Tyne before undertaking an inspection of Manx Airlines Isle of Man terminal at Ronaldsway Airport. The takeover was announced in April when Mr G H Drummond, Manx Airlines chairman, stated that his directors were satisfied that the sale was in the best interests of the Island and they felt that only a large organisation such as Silver City could provide the number of aircraft necessary to cope with the ever-increasing volume of traffic.

With the formalities over Manx Airlines, who retained its own identity, and Silver City then filed applications for new services, but whilst both applied for licences to run for a ten year period the Manx Airlines licence was for a passenger and freight service from Ronaldsway to Stranraer (Castle Kennedy) and Newtownards with Bristol Freighters and Dakotas, and Silver City's was for operating a vehicle, passenger and freight service on the same routes on the basis of one to twelve return flights a day. When permission was duly received from the MCTA in May for both companies to operate between the Isle of Man and Northern Ireland, with Silver City going to Newtownards and Manx Airlines to Nutts Corner, both were expected to introduce services before the July holidays so, anticipating an increase in the number of flights using Newtownards the owners, Messrs Short Brothers and Harland Ltd, agreed to extend the main runway by 250 yards to enable the landing of Superfreighter aircraft (the first of which landed on 10 May 1957 carrying a party from Queens University Athletic Club). Whilst the work was in progress Silver City obtained temporary permission to conduct their Stranraer service from the nearby Royal Naval Air Station at Sydenham from 17 May until Newtownards was again usable.

The decision to use Sydenham had been made back in 1953 after Air Commodore Powell had successfully discussed with the Admiralty the possibilities of using their airbase as an air ferry terminal. There were also difficulties in using Nutt's Corner, Belfast's principle civil airport since 1946, because of the limitations set by that airports single runway. Nevertheless, this latter consideration had not hindered the company's use of that site in July when, due to low cloud over Newtownards, a Freighter was diverted there with two cars and five passengers on board. On this occasion, and because there were no special loading ramps at the airport, the cars had to be driven from the aircraft onto a lorry and taken to one of the MTCA's automatic ramps to be lowered to the ground.

Manx Airlines, who operated services to Newcastle, Glasgow and Carlisle, was originally formed as Manx Air Charter in 1947 with one de Havilland Rapide, but after acquiring two more in the next six months (the company had four by 1952) services were first put on a scheduled basis in 1950 with a Ronaldsway to Carlisle service, followed in 1953 with extra services between Ronaldsway, Renfrew and Newcastle.

For their first experimental flights between Ireland and the Isle of Man Silver City initially instigated a twice-weekly freight service between Newtownards and Ronaldsway in May, carrying pork carcasses for the Belfast Fatstock Marketing Association. As to the vehicle ferry service, it was not until 11 July that an article appeared in the Irish News stating it would start operating between the two terminals on 3 August. Rates for this 25-minute service were £8-10s for cars, £2-10s for motorcycles, 4s for cycles and £2 (single) for passengers. However, with the development of the Suez crises for which, if the need arose, Mr Mekie had publicly made available 'all' the company's aircraft, and the violent storms throughout the British Isles at the beginning of August which would disrupt all services during the Bank Holiday period, it was decided to delay the Island's ferry service until the beginning of September when it was hoped to commence the operation to coincide with the opening of the Manx Grand Prix races.

Nevertheless, although the feasibility of such a service was shown by the popularity of their freight service, the fact that Manx Airlines had been promised Mk 170 Freighters to expand their services (two by the end of 1956) again forced Silver City to postpone the inauguration of the scheduled vehicle ferry operation not only due to a lack of aircraft but also because the summer season was coming to a close. There was also another matter that had been overlooked, and it was that another airline still operating into Ronaldsway had also obtained ATAC permission to run a vehicle ferry service between the Island and Belfast. This concern, Dragon Airways, had received approval in October 1954 to operate Mk 170s for a seven year period on a seasonal passenger, vehicle ferry and freight basis between Liverpool (Speke) and Belfast (Nutts Corner), with an intermediate stop on the Isle of Man at Ronaldsway, and had hoped to start this on 4 June 1955 to run from June to September inclusive each year.

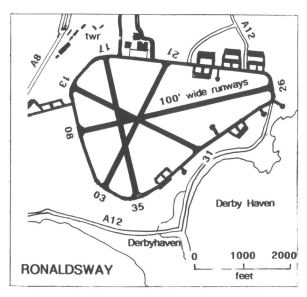

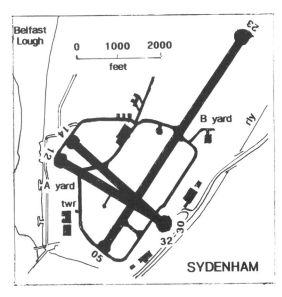

After the opening of their Southampton to Guernsey vehicle ferry service on 27 February the following month saw the creation of yet another seasonal service by Silver City in the form of a daily, ultra-cheap, combined road, air and rail express passenger service between Victoria Coach Station, London and Paris. Run in alliance with Samuelson New Transport Ltd, (a subsidiary of London Coastal Coaches Ltd, the owners of Victoria Coach Station), Compagnie Air Transport (Silver City's French associate), and the French Railways (SNCF), the service was christened the 'Silver Arrow'.

For the 'Silver Arrow' service passengers were required to report to Victoria Coach Station 15 minutes before being taken by 44-seat coach on the three-hour trip to Ferryfield. After a short break there for refreshments, they boarded a special 50-seat 'Silver Arrow Bristol Wayfarer', operated in conjunction with CAT, for the flight to Le Touquet. At Etaples railway station (for Le Touquet, and reached by a ten-minute bus journey from there) the passengers joined a French Railways luxurious high-speed buffet-equipped 50 or 60-seat 'Dietrich' Autorail diesel car by which they arrived at Gare du Nord station in the centre of Paris some 140 minutes later, after a scheduled 65 mile journey at a total elapsed time from city centre to city centre of six hours 50 minutes. Services left London at 0800 and 1400 hrs with the return services from Paris departing at 0930 and 1530 hrs, fares for the complete journey being £4-5s single and £8-10s return and included for up to 44 lbs of luggage, those joining at Ferryfield paid £4 single and £8 return.

On 17 May, the day <u>before</u> the official inaugural flight, a party of journalists were taken on a demonstration run along with Air Commodore Powell, Mr and Mrs W G Franklin, Group Captain W W Deane, Mr and Mrs Manley Walker, and Captain N Waugh who was in charge of the new service (it was stated that it would start first on 11th May then the 15th, however in the '*Air Ferry News*' June issue it was said to have started on the 17th!). The day coincided with the official opening of a new motel at Le Touquet for which M J H Sainsard, the airport manager and managing director of the new enterprise, was largely responsible.

By similar means the company also commenced a scheduled 'Silver Arrow' coach-air-coach service between Victoria Coach Station, via Lydd and Ostende, to Brussels, just four days before the Paris service, but this took seven hours 40 minutes from city centre to city centre. The operation was purely Silver City's own enterprise but basically an extension of Air Kruise's road-air-rail connections (on which they had hoped to use their Handley Page Herald), fares being £4-15s single and £7-1s return, with services leaving London at 1000 and Brussels at 1100 hrs.

Until May the new coach/air services used the existing terminal buildings at Ferryfield but as from the end of the month, when the new Air Kruise terminal became fully operational, these services were moved into that building which was capable of handling up to 2,000 passengers a day. The company name of 'Silver Arrow Ltd' was registered on 14 August 1956.

With a view to consolidating and expanding their position in the north-west corner of the British Isles, and as a way of acquiring more Dakotas, the BAS group then purchased the Lancashire Aircraft Corporation. At the time of amalgamation LAC operated out of Squires Gate, Blackpool over routes between Blackpool and Leeds to the Isle of Man and Jersey, as well as from Birmingham to the Isle of Man, using two Dakotas, two de Havilland Rapides and a four-engined DH86b (the same aircraft Chamberlain flew in to meet Hitler in Munich in 1938). Founded in January 1946 by Eric Rylands (the managing director of Skyways, the parent company of LAC), maintenance work was carried on by Salmesbury Engineering, also set up by Rylands in 1942, and heavy charter operations started early in 1947 from Bovingdon after LAC had purchased Halton freighters. By 1952, with their main base still at Blackpool, the company owned some 70-plus aircraft including 23 Yorks, six Haltons, 14 Rapides, eight Consuls and 21 various other types.

Following the takeover, the first news of which had been announced in December when Air Commodore Powell and other board members arrived in Blackpool to hold negotiations with LAC directors, it was agreed that BAS would allow LAC to retain its own identity within the

BAS group, and continue operations from Squires Gate using its own staff. The main aim was to improve the already adequate LAC services by integrating those which to date had been duplicated, and thus put the group in a more formidable position to increase the 60,000 or so passengers LAC had carried during the 1956 season. Notwithstanding this, by 1958 the company had been completely absorbed into the northern division of Silver City Airways with its services flying under the banner of the latter, and later the name of LAC was acquired by Salmesbury Engineering Company Ltd in connection with their purchase of the Edgar Percival Aircraft Company.

After the initial success of their vehicle ferry service to Guernsey a similar one for Jersey, but also with freight, was inaugurated by Silver City from Southampton. An earlier proving flight carried a Wolseley 15/50 and a ¼-ton Morris van for delivery to Cleveland Garages Ltd, the Nuffield distributors at Havre-des-Pas on the island, and the service itself started on 13 July. With a fare structure based on the Guernsey services it was approved to run until 30 September 1961, but initially a trial operation for two months up to 9 September was set up in conjunction with the company's Southampton to Guernsey service.

For this combined operation, the merits of which were made apparent in August when His Excellency the Lieut Governor of Jersey, Sir Gresham Nicholson arrived back on Jersey from the mainland with his car and family, the company's Freighters were routed through Southampton-Guernsey-Jersey-Southampton on Mondays, Wednesdays and Fridays and for the rest of the week flew the reverse route. The fare structure was based on that for the 1954 Southampton to Guernsey service.

By September, and with the winter season approaching, Silver City decided to apply a more radical approach to their Roadair service in an attempt to give their aircraft a greater rate of utilisation during the winter period. This cargo scheme had suffered in its early days mainly through the non-availability of aircraft, but was at last to fulfill its potential when the company introduced the idea on all but the Ostende services. This was achieved by linking Ferryfield with Calais and Le Touquet, and Southampton with Cherbourg, Deauville, Guernsey and Jersey. By December 1957 the service had been extended to include a direct scheduled London (Battersea) to Paris (Le Bourget) combined air and road service.

This increased operation coincided with MTCA approval in October for the company to run a vehicle ferry and freight service between Cherbourg and Guernsey and/or Jersey until 31 December 1961, and whilst the freight side of the operation had only been inaugurated in the second week of October a record tonnage of freight was flown between English, French and Channel Island airports, figures being 1,002 short tons in September, 3,055 in October and 4,188 in November, with livestock forming a large part of the October total. Further commodities flown in September and October included pottery, cheese, lingerie, lace, paper, radio and television sets, cine film, perfume, clothing, car spares, machine and tool parts, books, cutlery, electrical equipment and bicycles.

Although company operations were again quite prolific for the year of 1956 the vehicle and passenger totals carried were slightly down on the 1955 figures, being 44,848 vehicles (of which 33,191 were cars) and 125,243 passengers, this being due primarily to the company having announced a 15% increase in fares at the beginning of the year.

This increase, which had originated back in March 1955 when other IATA operators had raised fares by 15%, had been originally rejected by Silver City on the basis that 44% of their available aircraft space had already been sold, and it was felt that any increase would have singled out certain passengers. They had hoped that by the end of 1955 an increase could have been avoided, and the company's seven year record of constant fare reductions maintained, but costs rose rapidly and fares charged for 1956 were deemed quite economic.

Nevertheless this did not deter the company from breaking at least one of their records on 30 July when they beat their 24 month record of 222 crossings in a single day. On this day the Freighters flew to and from France and Belgium no fewer than 246 times, carrying 539 vehicles and 1,700 passengers. Under these circumstances a rapid turnaround was of the essence therefore, on taxying onto the pan after landing, aircraft requiring fuel would fly a blue flag from the cockpit window to speed up the refuellers' response to their needs. Normally the absolute emergency maximum number of crossings for the company's vehicle ferry operation was no more than 206 in a day, but gales which had swept Britain on Sunday 29 July halted all types of ferrying activities that day, accordingly from dawn the next day until the last aircraft landed at midnight (normally no night flying was done) the Freighters were landing and taking off every two minutes.

Speedy operations, particularly at turn-round, were critical and well-practised but every now and then something would throw everything out of gear. One example was a car driver at Le Touquet who was seen to be repeatedly topping up the brake fluid master cylinder whilst in the queue waiting to board, the reason for this became apparent after loading when the brakes failed and it crashed through the rear partition and into the passenger compartment!

The year again saw Ferryfield Airport handling more freight than any other British airport, with a total of 56,224 short tons exceeding even London Airports total of 44,508 tons by nearly 12,000 tons. Similarly the airport carried a large share of the country's passemgers with more than 159,507 passing through in over 24,000 aircraft movements, the most impressive month being November when movements increased by some 530% over the same period in 1955 with 2,356 landings and takeoffs made up in the main of Silver City freight services and Air Kruise Hungarian refugee flights. This month also boasted a 442% increase in the freight handled over the same period in 1955 with a total of 5,380 tons.

Silver City Airways - 1957

As a result of a revised rates structure at the beginning of this year Silver City were again able to reduce fares on their vehicle ferry services by, in some cases, up to 30% and actual single fare reductions ranged from 10s to £3-10s. Passenger rates remained unchanged as it was generally believed that the generous petrol allowances introduced on the Continent would cause the greatest exodus of British motorists since the war - in France for example each tourist received 44 one-gallon coupons on landing.

These new fares were only effective on the routes from Ferryfield to Calais, Le Touquet and Ostende, and from Southampton to Cherbourg and Deauville, the rates for vehicles being categorised into three distinct groups :-

A - for outward travel on Fridays, Saturdays, Sundays and Mondays in July and August and in late June and early September (applying over a total of 46 days),
B - for outward travel on certain midweek days in July and August, and during certain weekends in April, May, June, September and October (applying over a total of 102 days),
C - for outward travel every day in January, February, March, November and December and most midweek days in April, May, June, September and October (applying to cheap off-peak flights over the remaining 31 weeks of the year).

There were certain variations in the periods applying to each category for homeward travel but whether the real object of this fare structure, which had taken a few months to plan, was to confuse everybody, it was said that the new midweek category B was introduced to increase aircraft utilisation on those summer days when aircraft were not always full, whilst in reality it had only been adopted as a means of levelling out peak traffic.

An example of this new rate structure was that a Ford Prefect with two passengers flying midweek in August from Ferryfield to Le Touquet would cost just £27-2s return, instead of £29-12s in 1956, whilst during August weekends the flight cost was £28-12s. For this size of car the lowest off-season return fare was £13, exactly £2 less than in 1956. Also between these termini, a really large car of Bentley size also with two passengers was charged £52-2s return for midweek August travel compared with £59-12s previously, and early summer travel for the same car and passenges was £42-2s return instead of £55-12s.

Regarding motorcycles and the like, for these, sidecar outfits, scooters and three-wheelers, category A and B fares remained the same as the standard off-peak fares during 1956 but the new C schedule fares were reduced even more. An example of this was that the revised minimum return fare for a sidecar outfit flown from Lydd to Le Touquet was £6 as against £7 in 1956, with that for a 500cc motorcycle on the same route £5 instead of £5-10s. The rates for bicycles and tandems remained unchanged.

For the 1957 season Silver City also clarified the frequencies of their vehicle ferry services but, whilst there were some changes made, the services from Lydd to Calais, Le Touquet and Ostende, Southampton to Guernsey and Jersey, and from Stranraer to Belfast were run all year round (even though the latter route had just had 1s per mile added to its internal fuel tax rate). All the remaining routes, Southampton to Cherbourg and Deauville, and the envisaged Isle of Man to Belfast and Stranraer, were to be operated on a seasonal basis.

The Lydd to Le Touquet service was the busiest with a scheduled daily frequency of 60 return flights during the summer and provision for extra flights when necessary. On the next busiest route, Lydd to Calais, the frequency was marginally lower whilst the Lydd to Ostende route had upwards of two return flights a day, and the services from Southampton to Guernsey and Jersey were operated on a daily basis. The Stranraer to Belfast operation had a maximum frequency of 15 flights a day, and those between Southampton, Cherbourg and Deauville up to ten and three flights a day respectively. The proposed Isle of Man to Belfast and Stranraer route had, if it operated, just two return flights daily.

On 22 March it was announced that BAS had concluded an agreement to acquire Dragon Airways Ltd, a company operating out of Woolsington Airport, Newcastle. This privately-owned airline had been formed in 1954 and was formerly controlled by three organisations, Hunting Clan Air Transport, the Elder Dempster Shipping Group and Tyne Tees Shipping Company Ltd (a subsidiary of Coast Lines). With its fleet of two Herons, two Rapides, one Gemini and various other light aircraft it had operated scheduled services from Liverpool and Glasgow, and seasonal services from Stoke on Trent (Meir) to the Channel Islands and the Isle of Man, but in February 1957 suspended all its regular flights out of Newcastle.

It had been BAS's intention after the takeover to integrate the route network currently covered by Dragon Airways, namely Newcastle to Germany, Holland, Northern Ireland and Norway, with that of the northern division of their member company Silver City Airways, and in order to achieve this the airline was reorganised to utilise all its existing staff and re-named Silver City (Northern) Aviation Ltd. The new company undertook to commence inclusive tour flights between Newcastle and Bergen in addition to their regular routes to Amsterdam, Belfast, Dusseldorf and Stavanger and for this the two de Havilland Herons from Dragon were added to the northern fleet of Silver City.

With this latest acquisition into the BAS group, which already included Britavia Ltd, Silver City Airways, Aquila Airways, Air Kruise (Kent) Ltd, Manx Airlines, Ferry Airports Ltd and the Lancashire Aircraft Corporation, the group's activities over the next two years were quite formidable. Their fleet at this stage, comprising over 50 aircraft including 14 Bristol Superfreighters, eight Bristol short-nosed Freighters, seven Dakotas, five Hermes IVs, three Solents, two Herons, four Rapides and a de Havilland 86B, constituted Britains largest independant airline consortium.

The group's activity can be shown by the number of services operated by the individual airlines. In addition to Silver City's own services described earlier, and the then recent extension to their coach-air-rail services to Paris and Brussels which was now linked by coach services/tours operated by Linjebuss European Coach Services, the scope of their airline operations during this period was as follows:-

Britavia Ltd - from its base at Blackbushe it operated trooping flights to Aden, Bahrain, Colombo, Cyprus, East and West Africa, the Far East, Malta and Tripoli, inclusive tour services to Austria, Italy and Spain, and world-wide passenger and freight charters. During 1956 their Hermes aircraft carried 33,477 passengers and flew 1,623,332 miles. A travel agency (Britavia Travel Ltd) with licences for all major air and steamship companies was also owned by the company.

Silver City (Northern) Aviation - latterly Dragon Airways, operated from their base at Woolsington Airport, Newcastle scheduled passenger, freight and inclusive tour services to Amsterdam, Blackpool, Brussels, Dusseldorf, Hamburg and the Isle of Man, and between Leeds and Brussels.

Aquila Airways - from its Hamble base on Southampton Water it flew scheduled passenger services to Lisbon - Canary Islands; Marseilles - Capri/Ischia; Marseilles - Genoa; and to Genoa, Montreux and Santa Margerita.

Air Kruise - from Ferryfield it operated numerous seasonal inclusive tour and scheduled cross Channel passenger services as well as freight and charter flights. Scheduled routes were to Lyons as part of the 'Blue Arrow' coach-air-rail service between London and the Costa Brava, Cote d'Azur, Italy, Spain, the Mediterranean and French Alps; and to Calais, Jersey, Le Touquet and Ostende, all these being eventually incorporated into Silver City's passenger division in October 1957. The inclusive tours operated from Lydd with the very occasional departure from Blackbushe (and eventually also from Gatwick) to Basle, Jersey, Luxembourg, Lyons, Nice, Palma, Perpignan, Saltzburg and Toulouse; from Manchester or Newcastle to Basle, Luxembourg, Ostende and Stavenger; and from Leeds to Barcelona and Rotterdam.

Manx Airlines - from their base at Ronaldsway on the Isle of Man scheduled passenger, freight and coach-air services were operated as well as ambulance and short/long charter flights. Scheduled routes comprised services to Belfast, Carlisle, Edinburgh and Newcastle; and from Ronaldsway and Belfast to Stranraer, with a coach link to Glasgow.

Lancashire Aircraft Corporation - based at Squires Gate, Blackpool it operated scheduled passenger services as well as freight and passenger charter work. Its scheduled routes were from Blackpool and Leeds to the Isle of Man and Jersey; Blackpool to Belfast and Ostende; and Birmingham to the Isle of Man. This latter service was run in conjunction with British Railways who linked Blackpool with their stations throughout the north-west of England, the Midlands and London, and complimented LAC's existing coach-air Isle of Man operation.

It is worth mentioning that, on 17 April, Miss Pat Sanderson, a 21-year old Manchester secretary, was the 100,000th coach-air passenger to book an Isle of Man passage. As part of the celebrations she was a guest for two days of SCA, the Manx Tourist Board and 26 coach operators from all over the North of England.

Besides these developments to their passenger services Silver City had, at the beginning of 1957, re-organised their commercial departments by establishing two commercial divisions. For this, the first of many internal changes, the executives of the air ferry division mainly concerned with all the commercial activities relating to the company's air ferry and Silver Arrow services were Mr E Manley Walker, commercial manager, and Mr L McCracken, the reservations manager (formerly both the sales and reservations manager), assisted by Mr E A Ayres, reservations superintendent, and Mr J R Hawkes, the sales manager (formerly the assistant commercial manager, freight and charter division). Divisional sales representatives were also appointed to establish a closer liason with sales agents throughout the UK and to help them in increasing sales. For the freight and charter division the principle executive was Mr L R Pavey, commercial manager.

March also saw the announcement of a special one-day vehicle ferry service to run between Newtownards and Jurby (Isle of Man) on 7 July primarily for those attending the Jubilee year 'Senior TT' races. The service was to consist of eight close-knitted flights departing from

Newtownards at 0530, 0650, 0820, 0940, 1640, 1810, 1940 & 2100, and returning at 0605, 0725, 0855, 1015, 1725, 1845, 2015 & 2135 hrs, the return fares being £4-15s per head, £2-10s for autocycles and scooters, £3-10s for motorcycles up to 250cc and £4-10s over, whilst combinations were £5-10s.

Come the day however, the service was preceded five weeks previous by the consolidation of Silver City's intended daily 25-minute summer seasonal vehicle ferry service when, on 1 June, a Mk 21 flew from Newtownards to Ronaldsway with one car, six motorcycles and 20 passengers. Three more flights that same day carried four cars, 30 motorcycles and 90 passengers, most of whom were attending the TT motorcycle races on the island. The fares on this service were £2-13s single for passengers and from £9-10s for cars, £3-10s for motorcycles and 4s for bicycles.

After the establishment of this service, which by the end of August only warranted an on-demand operation, the groups' schedules out of Newtownards met with a setback in January 1958 when there were reports that the Newtownards to Stranraer vehicle ferry was to be withdrawn. This announcement had come about after Silver City suspended the service in November 1957 due to insufficient winter traffic to make it viable, although the intention was to resume the service in April 1958. However, with the company hoping to increase the number of Continental vehicle ferry passenger and freight flights, and the northern divisions' expansion programme including for passenger services between Newtownards and Blackpool, and Liverpool to the Isle of Man, together with the limitations of their fleet and the cost of keeping Castle Kennedy operative during the winter lay-off, it was felt that to continue the vehicle ferry into 1958 would be quite unrealistic. Castle Kennedy was therefore closed down and the Isle of Man to Newtownards vehicle ferry service suspended.

The effect of these decisions was far-reaching. In July 1957 Silver City had finally received MTCA approval to operate a vehicle ferry service between Stranraer and the Isle of Man up to 31 December 1961, but with the closure of Castle Kennedy this operation was never to take place. Additionally, Manx Airlines coach-air services between Renfrew, Ronaldsway and Newtownards, all routed through Castle Kennedy, had to be withdrawn - a fact that was to make them increase the frequency of their ordinary Renfrew to the Isle of Man service. However, the most significant result of the closure of Castle Kennedy and the cessation of the Stranraer to Newtownards vehicle ferry occurred on 15 April 1958 when Silver City moved their Northern Ireland headquarters from Newtownards to Nutts Corner. This move arose even after Short Brothers and Harland had decided to keep Newtownards open for a one year trial period, despite an earlier decision to close it after revenue lost through reduced operations by Silver City prevented them from providing a full-time fire fighting service.

A well-publicised charter in April 1957 was when a Silver City Freighter undertook seven flights between Southampton and Cherbourg with laundry and other ships stores for the Queen Mary, which had became strike-bound in France after having been blacked by dock unions from berthing at Southampton. However, the most publicised charter arose during the summer when a Mk 21 flew a Sikorsky S51 helicopter, G-AHJW, from Blackbushe to a specially-prepared airstrip at Mestervig, Greenland for use by a Danish mining company in transporting their ground surveyors, stores and technical equipment to inaccessible sites, in a similar manner to that carried out by Air Charter Ltd the previous summer.

On 14 July, the ninth anniversary of the first inaugural flight and a most auspicious date (Bastille Day), a company Mk 32 Freighter made the 100,000th in-service crossing of the English Channel when it flew from Lydd to Le Touquet with two cars and four passengers. In the whole year their ferry services carried 43,002 vehicles (of which 34,361 were cars) and 117,178 passengers, and flew a total of 73,000 tons of vehicles and freight across the Channel in a year that saw aircraft movements recorded every day at Ferryfield as the only airport in the British Isles not to be affected by fog.

Possibly the highlight of the season, as far as the company staff were concerned, was the continuation of challenge football matches between Ferryfield FC and Le Touquet (Paris-Plage

Airport) FC. The French team had won in 1956 with a goal aggregate of 4-1 and, with an aggregate of 7-1 in 1957, this rivalry continued for many years. The idea of these sporting interludes had originated at Lympne when foggy weather stopped services and, at the instigation of a HM Customs officer, a cricket team formed from airport employees started playing on the airfield grass in order to entertain frustrated passengers who were reluctant to divert to the boat ferries. The passengers made up the opposing team and it was not unusual on clear days, when there were no delays, for passengers checking in to enquire if a return match was on the cards. Known as 'The Ferryfielders', the Silver City cricket club lasted for many years and also played against the local clubs. Another item on the company social calendar at the end of the year was the choice of Miss Sally Harris, the 'air hostess with the mostest', as 'Miss British Aviation Services' for 1958.

Included amongst other diversions from scheduled services were the many films made in the UK and featuring the Bristol Freighter. One was the drama **'Man in the Sky'**, the stars of which included Jack Hawkins, Lionel Jeffries and Victor Maddern, in which G-AIFV, the 3rd Dalma Jain aircraft, was used intensively. Mid-week filming at Wolverhampton airport in May 1956 required pilot Eddie Ruecroft to carry out general flying, as well as having the cockpit in front of a moving cloudscape for ground 'flying' shots, and the rear door for a 'baleout' sequence. The aircraft was damaged after failing an overshoot on one engine but after being repaired returned to service until finally broken up in 1962. A Freighter made a brief appearance in the comedy film **'That Riviera Touch'** which starred Ernie Wise and Eric Morecambe, and we cannot forget the classic TV series **'Garry Halliday'** starring Terence Longdon & Terence Alexander (who later went on to play Charlie Hungerford for the series 'Bergerac') as a pair of go-anywhere freelance pilots.

In 1957 Silver City once more carried royalty, if you consider the Queen's Rolls Royce car to be just that. In fact they did three such trips, in April one was flown from Lydd to Le Touquet in readiness for its use in Paris during the state visit to France, the others being taken from Southampton to Jersey and Guernsey in July. Returning to the house-moving theme, on 16 December the last charter of the year saw Freighter G-AGVC fly an Isle of Man coastguard from Newtownards to the island along with his family and domestic effects when he was transferred for a period of special duty at Ardglass.

Nevertheless, 1957 brought unfortunate news when it was reported in September that, due to ill health, Air Commodore Powell would resign as managing director with effect from 31 December. Although there were strong rumours that more was underfoot than was obvious from the official statement, after this most regretful news – the outcome of which certainly sealed Aquila's and Silver City's future fate – Silver City's vehicle ferry operations during the year nevertheless still made history.

Silver City Airways – 1958

In order to win traffic from other airlines and the ship ferrying companies, all of whom were raising their rates, further reductions on the company's cross-Channel ferry charges had been announced in December 1957 for the 1958 summer season. On average the fares had cuts of around 25% on the 1957 summer rates, while in the case of some popular cars there were savings of almost half, and for nearly every class of car there would be reductions between the peak period from June to September. To achieve these rates, applicable only on the Lydd to Calais, Le Touquet and Ostende, and the Southampton to Cherbourg and Deauville services, the peak summer period which had consisted of 46 days for outward travel and 30 for inward travel were amended to apply on only 17 days in each direction.

An example of these changes was that the standard single fare on the Calais or Le Touquet service for a small family car up to 12'-0" in length became £5-10s, compared with the minimum of £6-10s and a peak fare of £8-10s in 1957. The new peak fare was also £1-10s cheaper at £7, and a larger car such as a Rover 105 had a standard summer fare of £11-10s single as against £12-10s, and a peak fare of £13-10s instead of £17 the year before. Before

1 June and after 31 October (in fact since 1 October 1957) fares were cheaper still with no peak fares at the busy Easter and Whitsun weekends, whereas in 1957 these higher rates applied to 34 days. An off-season single fare for the same small car up to 12'-0" in length was £4 as against the 1957 rate of £6-10s. Passenger fares did go up slightly from £2-18s to £3 for the single rate, a change brought about by a tax increase in French airports.

Following the introduction of these rates there was one significant revision to them for the Lydd to Ostende service, applicable from 1 April to 30 September, which came about after objections from Sabena who operated in association with Air Charter Ltd on their Southend to Ostende vehicle ferry service. As a result of this, cars of 13'-6" long and upwards had to be carried at the standard rate and those over 15'-0" long at the peak season rate, but bicycle, motorcycle and passenger rates were unaffected.

As for Silver City's passenger network expansion from Newcastle, in the summer of 1958 there were just 13 weekly flight schedules operating, made up of four international and two internal routes. Inaugural flights for the internationals were made on 5 May to Amsterdam for Mondays and Thursdays, and to Dusseldorf for Mondays, flight time to Amsterdam being 2¼ hours with fares of £21-10s return and £12 single whilst for Dusseldorf it was 3¼ hours at £27 and £15 respectively. A twice-weekly service to Brussels commenced on Thursdays and Fridays from 6 May, direct from Newcastle the flight took 3¾ hours with fares of £21 return and £11-13s single, but from an intermediate stop at Leeds the flight was 2¾ hours with fares of £17-10s and £9-14s respectively. The company also anticipated operating a 4¾-hour Thursday service to Hamburg with fares at £33-2s return and £18-8s single, but no record of this having taken place has been found.

The internal services went over to Blackpool and the Isle of Man, and were inaugurated on 18 and 24 May respectively. Fares on the daily Blackpool service were £4-15s return and £3-5s single, while on the five-day Isle of Man service which ran from Friday to Monday inclusive and on Wednesdays the fare was £6-5s return and £3-10s single.

On 4 May Silver City had introduced the first international air link with Blackpool when a once-weekly service to Ostende was started. The operation ran on Sundays with a 2½-hour flight time and fares at £15-14s return and £8-13s single. Other services inaugurated were between Edinburgh and the Isle of Man, on 1 June, and the Blackpool to Belfast route on 12 June, one month later than the expected start date of 17 May. The Edinburgh service operated on Fridays and Sundays with fares of £8-15s return and £5-5s single, whilst the Belfast service operated from Fridays to Sundays with only a return fare at £6-18s, except on Saturdays when this increased to £7-18s.

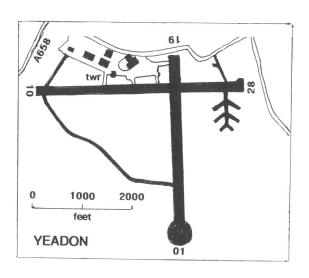

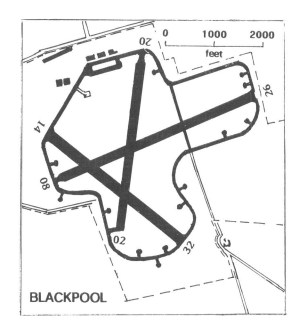

59

After consolidation on these routes, for which the Blackpool to Belfast run used the Bristol Wayfarer, the Edinburgh to Isle of Man the Heron or Wayfarer, and on all the others the Dakota, Silver City's southern divisions were also updating their services. On 21 May the twice-daily, 44-seat capacity coach-air-rail 'Silver Arrow' service betwen London and Paris was replaced by a once-daily 100-passenger schedule by which the journey from Victoria Coach Station to Ferryfield was carried out by three coaches in convoy. The air trip to Le Touquet was operated by two aircraft flying five minutes apart, one of which was Silver City's first Super-Wayfarer, G-AMWA, converted to a 60-seat all-passenger configuration and finished in a new livery of blue and silver with white topsides. The final stretch of the journey from Le Touquet to Paris was carried out as before. This service, for which fares were £8-19s return and £4-19s single with reductions of 11s and 6s-6d respectively for passengers joining at Ferryfield, left London at 0900 and arrived at Paris at 1650, with the return service leaving Paris at 1027 to arrive back at Victoria at 1800 hours.

March had further seen the expansion of Silver City's vehicle carrying capability when the Renault car company signed a one year agreement to fly all their type 750 and Fregate cars across the Channel for sale in this country, and in May Massey-Harris-Ferguson used the 'Roadair' service to reduce the delivery time for their tractor and implement spares from Manchester to Paris from one week to 72 hours, but perhaps the crowning point of the company's drive to increase the available services by which British export cars could be delivered to the Continent was in November when they introduced an extension to the 'Roadair' service to allow cars to be delivered to any town in Belgium, Germany, Holland and Switzerland. The principle of this was that cars would be delivered to Ferryfield in the normal way and flown on a regular ferry flight to Le Touquet, from where they were then conveyed to their ultimate destination on five to eight-car capacity road transporters under contract to Silver City.

Previous to this the company had further extended the 'Roadair' service when, in the last week of July, they introduced a new thrice-weekly freight schedule between their London freight depot near Chelsea Bridge and the Lille, Roubaix and Tourcoing areas of France. This service, run in conjunction with the road haulage company of Vepraet Patoux & Cie in Tourcoing, had departures scheduled to leave London at 1600 on Mondays and Thursdays to arrive at Tourcoing at 0200 the next day. On return the operation departed from Lille at 0900 on Mondays, Wednesdays and Fridays to arrive in London at 2200 the next day.

The most publicised charter carried out by Silver City in 1958 was for a 10'-0" long, one-man midget submarine brought across the Channel for undersea cable and survey work off Dungeness by the French underwater photographer and scientist M. Dmitri Rebikoff, the cost of a one-way ticket being just £2-14s-6d! In the same year the company Freighter G-ANWM was in the news twice; the first in May when it delivered two dismantled French Sud-Aviation Djinn midget gas-turbine helicopters into Ferryfield for European Helicopters Ltd to use in crop spraying trials, and the second in October when it carried a 60'-0" long racing shell from the University of Washington Rowing Club, plus a similar boat belonging to a Russian crew, from Blackbushe to Helsinki.

Altogether the most significant event of 1958 was on Monday 14 July when Silver City celebrated its 10th anniversary. On this day, which was more by way of a fitting tribute to the inventiveness and creativity of 'Taffy' Powell who even had the foresight to start his invasion of the Continent on Bastille Day, it was intended to fly his original Armstrong Siddeley car to Le Touquet in the company's first ferrying Freighter, G-AGVC. Although the current owner of HXN 88, a Mr Galliford of Epsom, was eventually found only after a national newspaper campaign the previous December he arrived too late to connect with the flight and had to be flown over with his family on another aircraft.

The first part of the anniversary celebrations began just before 1000 at Ferryfield when over 80 journalists and company officials assembled, some having flown in from Gatwick and France. They watched the Mayor of Le Touquet, Dr J Pouget, wearing his tri-colour sash of office, unveil the English name 'the Fourteenth of July' on the starboard nose side of the new

"THE FOURTEENTH OF JULY" was the name of the flagship of Silver City Airways, which was unveiled by the Mayor of Le Touquet, Dr. J. Pouget, at Ferryfield, on Monday. On the right stands the Mayor of Lydd, who performed a similar ceremony at Le Touquet when he unveiled the port side of the aircraft, where the name is written in French.

Silver City Airways' 10th anniversary

Phenomenal growth of Kent airport

YET another milestone in the history of Kent's youngest but world-wide known airport was reached on Monday.

It was the tenth anniversary of Silver City Airways cross-Channel ferry.

The occasion was duly celebrated with ceremonies at Ferryfield, Lydd, and Le Touquet, where the town was also celebrating the national holiday, Bastille Day, which commemorates the establishment of the First Republic.

The first celebration on this side was the unveiling of the name on the starboard side of the company's flag-ship, a super Bristol freighter, drawn up outside the Ferryfield lounge. This ceremony was performed by the besashed Mayor of Le Touquet, Dr. J. Pouget.

He was introduced by Mr. Eoin C. Mekie, the company's chairman, who reminded the large gathering of British and French journalists that it was most appropriate that the anniversary fell on July 14th.

They were honoured by having Dr. Pouget with them, for he had done a great deal for their service and they were asking him to unveil the name of the flag-ship of the car ferry service.

APTLY NAMED

When unveiled, it was revealed that the flag-ship was aptly named "The Fourteenth of July."

Back inside the airport buildings Mr. Mekie read a good will message from a well known mem-

THE MAYOR OF LYDD, Alderman Gordon T. Paine, cuts the anniversary cake.

Pouget, who, speaking in English, hoped he would be invited to the 20th anniversary celebration in 1968, M. Jean Sainsard, Director-General of Le Touquet Airport.

TEN YEARS OF CHANNEL AIR FERRYING

It was a day of ceremony, of popping champagne corks and of flowing oratory — on both sides of the Channel.

Silver City Airways —whose headquarters are now in the Brompton Road at Knightsbridge — celebrated Bastille Day with an elaborate celebration of its own to mark the tenth anniversary of its cross-Channel air ferry.

Ten years ago to the day Silver City Airways flew a motor car (HXN 83) in a single Bristol Freighter across the Channel from Lympne to Le Touquet. Thus was inaugurated an all-British venture still not imitated by any other nation.

UNVEILING

The celebrations began just before 10 a.m., when the Mayor of Le Touquet, wearing his Tricolour sash of office, arrived at Ferryfield. After clearing the Customs, he unveiled the starboard nameplate of a Bristol Super Freighter which was revealed as "Fourteenth of July".

Dr. Pouget was presented with a silver salver by Mr. Eoin C. Mekie, C.B.E., chairman of Silver City Airways, as a token of the airline's grati-

the Casino de Foret for an excellent turbot and chicken lunch — and more champagne.

FIGURE-NOTE: In the ten years it has been in existence Silver City have carried 215,000 cars, 70,000 cycles and motorcycles and 759,000 passengers.

On the 10th anniversary of the vehicle air ferry many newspapers carried articles on SCA; the main one showing the unveiling of G-ANWK at Lydd is from the Kentish Times with the other from the Middlesex Independent & West London Star, both dated 18 July 1958.

61

The Mayor of Southend, Alderman Mrs C Leyland OBE, JP, watches her car being loaded into CAB Freighter Mk 31E G–AMLP at Southend on 17 October 1955 for shipment to Ostend. This was part of the inaugural celebrations for the new route, and not the only time the Mayor's car made this sort of journey (photo by Richardsons).

Members of the Calais Chamber of Commerce and CAB officials in the booking hall at Southend on 4 August 1958 during a visit with a view to making changes at Calais Airport in the way that vehicle ferry traffic was handled. With them, in uniform, is airport commandant Bernard Collins (photo by Geroy). Delegates from Rotterdam also visited on 3 October for similar reasons as Southend was something of a model for improvements.

Cheaper rates for shipping freight could be had at night. In this 1957 shot lettuces from Holland are being off-loaded from CAB Freighter Mk 31 G-ANMF 'Victory' at Southend straight onto the lorry for their Spitalfields market destination (photo by Richardsons).

CAB Freighters Mk 32 G-AMLP, 'NVR & 'NVS on the apron at Calais in August 1958 (via Arthur Leftley)

Two-wheeled machines were also accommodated. In this photo two newly-registered Royal Enfield Constellation motorcycles, one fitted with panniers and fairings, the other 'straight from the factory', are wheeled into CAB Freighter Mk 32 G-ANVR 'Vigilant' at Southend for the start of a Continental holiday (photo by Richardsons).

flagship, Freighter Mk 32, G-ANWK. The entire party was then received in the airport lounge where the Mayor of Lydd, Alderman G T Paine, cut the anniversary cake inscribed 'Silver City Air Ferry 1948-58'. Mr Mekie also presented Dr Pouget with a silver salver to mark the company's appreciation of his town's assistance over the past ten years. After this, and for the second part of the celebrations, the main contingent then proceeded to Le Touquet in the flagship and another aircraft where, after being greeted by the town brass band, Alderman Paine duly returned the honours by unveiling the French name 'la Quatorze Juillet' on the port nose side of the flagship. During lunch in the local casino Mr Mekie then presented a similar salver to Alderman Paine.

With regard to general activities of the group during 1958, back in May the Lydd Town Council had objected to a proposal by Ferry Airports Ltd that Ferryfield should be shown on the valuation list as a freight transport hereditament, with a corresponding reduction in rateable value. This application was quite understandable in view of the airport's increased freight intake, but the council viewed that this could not be so within the meaning of Section 5 of the Rating and Valuation (Apportionment) Act of 1928. Indeed this policy of refusing the use of Ferryfield for anything other than an airport or airfield was to prevent any future development of the site.

With this sobering thought out of the way Silver City's operations for the year were again to resume an upward trend by the beginning of June when they received their 40,000th car booking compared with 21,741 in 1957. Between 1 October 1957 and 31 March 1958 they had carried 7,698 cars and 17,830 passengers, compared to 4,145 and 10,593 respectively for the same period in 1957, and 5,434 and 14,950 in 1956. In August alone they carried a total of 11,720 cars and 2,350 other vehicles, and in total for the year that ended on 30 September they uplifted some 50,006 cars, 4,826 motorcycles, 1,200 bicycles and 153,760 passengers across in 23,042 trouble-free flights. Of the traffic flown, that carried on the Calais and Le Touquet services matched the airlines' expectations, while on the Cherbourg, Deauville and Ostende routes figures were 20%, 25% and 35% respectively above target.

In retrospect 1958 was the end of a sad period for the BAS Group. On 15 November 1957 one of the Aquila Airways Solents had crashed just over nine minutes after taking off from Southampton, with a loss of 46 lives, then on 27 February 1958 a Manx Airlines Freighter Mk 21, G-AICS, en route from Ronaldsway to Manchester crashed at Winter Hill some five miles south-east of Chorley, Lancashire with the loss of 35 of its 42 occupants, and to add fuel to the flames was the memory of Britavia's Hermes, G-ALDJ, that had crashed near Bournemouth on 5 November 1956 with the loss of seven, plus the Channel Airways Dove, G-AOCE, that had force-landed on the beach at Dungeness on 15 January 1958.

Although the Dove was operated by a separate company it was unfortunate that all the crashes occurred just before a House of Commons debate in which some strong criticism of the credibility, efficiency and safety of independent airlines was questioned during a private members motion designed to encourage independent airline operators. Earlier there had even been talk of legislation to stiffen the codes by which the life expectancy of wooden aeroplanes and flying boats was measured. This last event, however, was of no consequence to Aquila Airways who had concluded their last in-service operation on 30 September when their Solent flying boat 'Awatere' returned to Southampton from Madeira and moored in the notorious berth 50 (once used by the RMS Titanic).

Silver City Airways - 1959

By the close of 1958, which had seen the group formally open their brand new six-storey headquarters 'Silver City House' at 62 Brompton Road, London SW3 on 9 April, to replace their former registered premises at 1 Great Cumberland Place, London W1, the company again announced further fare reductions for the coming year's vehicle ferry services. From 1 October they had already cut the cross Channel rates by up to 25%, following the trial reductions during the same period in 1957/58 which had boosted their spring and winter traffic by 99%. These new cuts meant that for the first time the cost of ferrying a car of less than eleven feet in length to the Continent via the Le Touquet route was only £3-10s, exactly 10s less than on a similar-routed boat ferry.

These concessions were applicable on the routes until 31 May 1959, and were then followed by further reductions effective from 1 June. From that date until 30 September a summer fare in force for medium and small cars on the Ferryfield to Le Touquet service was up to 27½% less than that for 1958. Additionally, on the Ferryfield to Ostende, and Southampton to Cherbourg routes there were even greater cuts by up to 37½%, and whilst on the peak weekends slightly higher rates applied these were still cheaper than the peak fares in 1958.

An example of these reductions was that during the off-peak periods the single fare for a Morris Minor on the Le Touquet service was £5 as against £6-10s in 1958. For an Austin A35 using the Cherbourg and Ostende routes during the off-peak periods the charge was £5 instead of £8 in 1958, whereas if the same car was taken across in the peak period it cost £8 instead of £10.

The year had opened with reports of an experimental period of cheap day, 'no passport' air trips to France. The idea, something that the boats of Eagle Steamers had been operating for some four years from Clacton, Deal, Gravesend, Margate, Ramsgate and Southend to Boulogne and Calais, stipulated that British subjects or those from the Irish Republic need only use identity cards in lieu of passports, and had come about following talks between the British Home Office and the French Government. Although Silver City were not to be the first to introduce this facility, the honour having fallen to Air Charter Ltd at Southend, the company did provide the service on their Ferryfield to Le Touquet route between 31 March and 30 September, the return fares being £3-5s for adults and £1-15s for children.

A further development inaugurated on 2 June extended this service to include London with adult fares at £3-15s-6d, and children £2-0s-3d, running on Tuesdays, Wednesdays and Thursdays. Designated the 'Wheels and Wings' service the schedules were:-

Depart London Victoria Coach Station	0700	Depart Le Touquet	1830
arrive Ferryfield	1000	arrive Ferryfield	1850
depart Ferryfield	1030	depart Ferryfield	1930
arrive Le Touquet	1050	arrive London Victoria Coach Station	2230

For this service all seats were bookable in advance, however for normal scheduled vehicle ferry services seats could only be made available if they were not required by passengers travelling with their cars. Also, 'no passport' passengers could not fly on scheduled ferry flights leaving Ferryfield between 0830 and 1100 hrs, or return flights from Le Touquet between 1630 and 1900 hrs.

At the same time as the 'no passport' trips were publicised Silver City were also becoming involved with another concept concerning a new type of inclusive tour holiday being offered by Millbanke Tours (operators of Flair Holidays). For this clients were supplied with either a Ford Consul or Prefect car, all travel documents, route maps, a tank full of petrol, plus petrol coupons and hotel accommodation in either France, Italy or Spain. After receiving the car, which was delivered free to any address within 25 miles of London or handed over at a convenient railway station or airport for provincial clients, they made their way to Ferryfield from where Silver City flew them to Le Touquet for the start of their holiday.

Towards the end of February Silver City also gained permission, along with Skyways, to operate out of the former Battle of Britain airfield at Manston, near Ramsgate. This airfield possessed one of the world's longest runways, some 9,200 ft long by 750 ft wide, was still equipped with the fog dispersal system FIDO, and had been used by the USAF from 1950 to 1958 when it was returned to the Air Ministry. It was noted back in November 1958 of Silver City's interest in the airfield, when they had applied to the ATAC for permission to use Manston as an alternative terminal for their cross-Channel services due to Ferryfield working up to capacity at peak times. Indeed it was considered that, in propagating any future expansion programmes, use of the airfield would be inestimable.

With this background, and by way of bettering their previous coach-air-rail operation, the company inaugurated a new rail-air-rail London to Paris 'Silver Arrow' service via Manston on 15 June using the 68-seater Handley Page Hermes aircraft. The service was operated in association with British and French railways, on the British side it involved a train journey on British Railways' newly-completed electrified link between Victoria Station, London and Margate (or Birchington), whilst on the French side the journey between Etaples station at Le Touquet and the Gare du Nord, Paris was as before. The rest of the journey between rail terminals and airports was conducted by bus although plans were in hand to have rail spurs constructed to new stations at both Manston and Le Touquet airports.

On the day of the first service, which had been preceded by a proving flight on 25 May, the ex-Britavia Hermes, G-ALDP, now in Silver City colours and carrying just twenty-six passengers in rear-facing seats (having previously been used on trooping operations), was seen off by a group of company officials, local dignitaries and journalists, who afterwards were taken across to Le Touquet in another Hermes for the inaugural lunch and inspection of the facilities at that airport. Incredibly though, and despite a 50-minute saving on the previous London to Paris operation, the company were obliged to maintain exactly the same rates as 1958, namely £8-19s return and £4-19s single with passengers joining at Manston charged £8-8s and £4-12s-6d respectively. Children under 12 years of age were charged £4-9s-6d, £2-9s-6d, £4-4s and £2-3s-6d, and those under three 17/11d, 9/11d, 16/10d and 9/3d respectively. The service also departed from both London and Paris as for the 1958 operation but arrived at Paris at 1640 and London at 1705 hrs, the aircraft departing and arriving at Manston at 1240 and 1410 hrs respectively.

As to the operations of Silver City's northern passenger division, after a proving flight in April the company (in conjunction with Aer Lingus) inaugurated a new 58-minute service from Blackpool to Dublin, from where it connected to New York and Boston. This new service started on 15 May using either a 36-seat Dakota or the 16-seat Heron and ran on a twice-weekly basis on Fridays and Saturdays up to 1 June, from when it stepped up to four flights a week on Wednesdays and Fridays to Sundays inclusive. Fares were £4-18s single and £8-17s return with an additional return fare of £6-15s on all flights in May, June, September and October, and on Wednesday flights in July and August. The service was retained during the winter periods with flights operated by Aer Lingus on Fridays and Silver City on Mondays only.

Blackpool was linked with Newcastle on 2 October when the company introduced a new combined service from Newcastle to Amsterdam and Dusseldorf. This operation superceded similar services in 1958 and was operated on Mondays and Fridays with Dakotas, giving passengers the opportunity of flying between the two English airports for a 'same-day' return fare of £3-9s-6d.

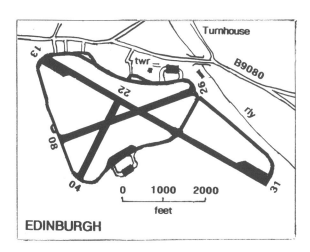

EDINBURGH

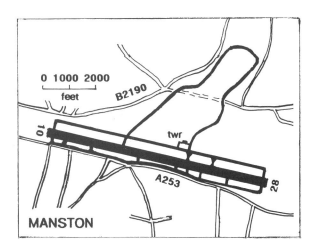

MANSTON

With regard to the company's vehicle-ferry operations during 1959, these services were again nationally highlighted during a six-week temporary closure of Eastleigh Airport due to necessary drainage works. The Cherbourg service, re-introduced on 11 March, had to be resumed from Hurn Airport, Bournemouth as did the seasonal Deauville service on 4 June. At this time BEA, Jersey Airlines and Cambrian Airways also operated from Hurn, but this situation was not new, having been experienced the previous Christmas when Eastleigh had been almost unusable through waterlogging, and this continued until 13 June, the day before regular services restarted from Eastleigh. Although used throughout the summer Eastleigh was again found unsuitable on 18 November for a new winter extension to their previous Southampton to Jersey vehicle ferry and the company again transferred its services to Hurn. BEA had objected to this operation as fares offered by Silver City were too low and therefore from 5 October it was re-routed via Cherbourg, although Silver City's administrative staff remained at Eastleigh until suitable accommodation was available at Hurn.

Apart from the vehicle ferry aspect the new re-routed cargo and freight/vehicle ferry service, which operated initially thrice-weekly on Mondays, Wednesdays and Fridays and used the airlines' existing service between Eastleigh and Cherbourg, provided Jersey farmers and nurseryman with a fast and efficient air link to get their produce to French and English markets. Passenger single fares were £3 and £1-10s for children, cars were rated at £3-10s for up to 11'-0", £5 up to 12'-6", £7-10s up to 13'-6", £10-10s up to 14'-6", and £12-10s up to 15'-6". Bicycles and mopeds under 100cc cost 2/6d, scooters and motorcycles under 250cc were £1 and £2 respectively and combinations £3-10s. Return fares were double the single rate, and the journey time from Jersey to Cherbourg took just 20 minutes.

In September the company announced further fare reductions for the off-peak vehicle ferry services with immediate effect and until 31 May 1960 of up to 40% for cars and 50% for other vehicles. An example of these was that the cost of flying a Morris Minor between Lydd and Calais or Le Touquet was reduced by 14% from £3-10s to £3, or to Ostende a reduction of 9% brought the price down from £4-10s to £4. The cost of flying a medium-sized car was also reduced from £13 to £9, a 31% cut, but the greatest bargain was the transportation of bicycles and mopeds (up to 1000cc) for which a 50% reduction over the previous winter rate was applied, the new rate being just 2/6d.

Of the notable bookings during the year, the most disturbing was when it was realised that a certain Mr G Fawkes was down to be flown between Lydd and Le Touquet with his car and three passengers on, of all days, 1 April, but to the relief of all the gentleman turned out to be the Reverend E G D Fawkes of Compton rectory, Winchester, Dorset. That same day Mr Artie Shaw, a Vespa dealer from Welling, Kent, beat the time for British Railway's 'Golden Arrow' service to Paris by 50 minutes while riding a Vespa Clubman scooter. With journalist friend Brian Collins he had left Victoria Station, London, at the same time as the boat train and travelled via Silver City's Lydd to Le Touquet ferry to arrive in Paris at 1950 GMT, in good time to meet another member of the team who had previously left on the 'Golden Arrow' from London at 1300 hrs.

Silver City was in the news in April when they carried for the first time three Shetland ponies on the newly-improvised Hurn to Cherbourg route, and in July when they airlifted some 300 Simca cars from France to Ferryfield for the Chrysler Organisation. Paris was again the destination in May when their Mk 32, G-AMWF, carried Rolls Royce's original 1906 Silver Ghost between Lydd and Le Touquet, this vehicle being en route to the capital so that it could be driven down the L'avenue des Champes-Elysees at the head of an entire cavalcade of Rolls Royces.

As to Silver City's 'Roadair' service, in April the company had announced cheaper rates and faster deliveries for their Belgium operation, the new tariff for the transportation of one ton of freight between London and Courtrai being revised from £37-10s to £22-10s, and from London to Brussels from £37-10s to £26-10s. Previous to this, and in conjunction with Sun/Air Holidays (Golden Coach Tours) Ltd, the company operated either Dakotas or Freighters between Lydd or Gatwick and Lyons at a frequency of one return flight weekly between 15 May and 19 October. Also in April the company had applied to the ATAC for permission to operate, from spring 1960, a normal scheduled service for the carriage of passengers, supplementary freight and mail, as well as a vehicle ferry, between Valley or Mona (on Anglesey) and Dublin. The first such application followed soon after news of a similar application having been made by Aer Lingus to operate a passenger service between Dublin and Valley, but met with a major snag when the RAF announced in the following January (1960) that no civilian aircraft could use Valley after March 1960. The project was therefore cancelled, although 1 September had been given as the most likely starting date.

In May Silver City had also applied for licences to operate deep-penetration vehicle ferry services from either Lydd or Manston to Paris (actually to Cormeilles, north-west of the city), as well as Auxerre (105 miles south-south-west of Paris) and Cologne. For a long time now they had contemplated such routes and it was now felt that traffic on the shorter routes warranted them running a limited number of off-season and night flights to inland Continental airports, especially as it was considered that the proposed fares would make good sense to the motorist. Previously they had always believed that these services would be fundamentally uneconomical unless realistic rates could be charged, so with this in mind the services were planned to utilise spare aircraft hours, times which could not have been economically available in earlier years. The routes approved were - Lydd and/or Manston to Cologne for a period up to and including 31 March 1961, and to Troyes and Pontoise (for Paris) for a period up to and including 31 March 1968.

The plan was to commence these routes in September 1959 and run over the winter period into the spring of 1960, but while it had been hoped to use the Mk 32 Freighter as before these aircraft were not really suitable for such long-range flights. As mentioned previously, the relationship between operating costs and the cargo carried increased substantially with distance, and the Freighter could therefore be considered uneconomic when flying in excess of 1270 miles (if air tariffs were directly proportional to those charged on shorter routes). Whilst Silver City were sincere in their desire to open these routes, and indeed eventually gained ATAC approval to operate them once their application (as well as a similar one by Channel Air Bridge) was rationalised by the Ministry, the scheme's ultimate feasibility really relied on the use of a newly-designed long-haul aircraft.

Murmerings of a new vehicle-ferry aircraft...

Whilst Silver City were sticking firmly to using the Bristol Freighter in various ways on all possible routes, and no moves whatsoever were being made towards acquiring a newer and more suitable type to operate services over the 'deep penetration' routes, their nearest competitor, British United Air Ferries, was looking to its own future in a positive way. Although they were already operating various other types as well as the Freighter BUAF's management had come to the same conclusion about the service life of the type on vehicle-ferry work and its inability to cope with varying route requirements, but had a more hardened attitude about the future of vehicle ferry operations, which would cease to exist with the eventual and inevitable retirement from service of the Bristol Freighter.

With the benefit of a far-seeing MD in the form of Freddie Laker, as well as an associate design and engineering company (Aviation Traders Engineering Ltd), BUAF were making definite moves to replace the Freighter as soon as possible so that longer routes, as well as the short cross-Channel hops, could be catered for. As with the Freighter freight was to be carried in lieu of empty car space in order to offset operating costs, although it was recognised that a greater vehicle payload would result in higher dividends on the longer routes. BUAF was looking for a 4-engined type, one with the right fuselage cross-section and cubic density and one that would be relatively cheap to produce for the somewhat specialised vehicle/freight ferry role.

At Laker's insistence ATEL chief designer Arthur Leftley set about converting the Douglas C54 to fit the role. The ideal points about the C54 were that it had already been proved in service for many years, the powerplants were easily obtainable, the type had a fail-safe wing structurer and, most critical from a sale point of view, used examples were relatively cheap to obtain for conversion. Design studies began in 1959, a mock-up layout was soon produced, and the first aircraft flew in June 1961 before being accepted into airline service in March 1962, where it immediately proved itself in the vehicle-ferry role.

Silver City Airways - 1959 (contd)

Notwithstanding the question mark hanging over the deep-penetration routes, 1959 actually turned out to be a better year for Silver City than 1958, for by the end of January 17,416 bookings had been received compared with 12,043 in 1958 (representing a 45% increase), whilst in the last week of January alone 3,540 cars were booked in 5½ working days, when compared with the previous weekly record of 2,600 bookings.

On 29 May Silver City's Mk 32, G-ANWH, with Captain Rosser at the controls, carried the 250,000th car, a Sunbeam Rapier between Lydd and Le Touquet. On this trip the car's occupants, Mr & Mrs H L Kent and Mr & Mrs Milner of Sutton Coldfield, were en route to Spain and surprised on collecting their tickets to be met by W/C Kennard who promptly reimbursed their £38 fare and presented them with four overnight bags, souvenir key-rings and a Silver City Airways car badge.

With the carriage of this car Silver City had, since 1948, made over 146,000 flights to and from the European mainland and carried over 856,900 passengers and 71,180 motorcycles and bicycles. Also in the 12 months ending 30 June they had carried 67,452 cars, 193,142 passengers in 28,973 flights and 103,699 tons of freight on their vehicle-ferry services but an article in 'The Times' of 22 April 1960 had much reduced figures. On 18 September the company carried its one millionth air ferry passenger, and accordingly 13-year old Nicholas Malcolmson of Bristol was presented with a leather cased pen and pencil set, his younger sister receiving a doll as the 1,000,001st passenger.

Undoubtably though, by 1959 the company had established itself as a household name, especially in the light of their recent involvement in the filming of such TV personalities as Harry Corbett (with Sooty and Sweep), Dixon of Dock Green and Garry Halliday. In October the airline sponsored its second motor car event when the Silver City Trophy was raced at Snetterton in Norfolk; won by Ron Flockhart in 39 minutes and 49 seconds, the average speed for his BRM over 25 laps of the 2.7-mile long circuit was 101.71 mph. The third event for the company was a 132-mile Formula 1 trophy held at Brands Hatch in Kent on August Bank Holiday Monday, 1960; won by Jack Brabham in a Cooper-Climax at a time of one hour 25 minutes and 36.6 seconds, Graham Hill (winner of the first company-sponsored race held at Brands Hatch on Boxing Day, 1959, when driving a Lotus in a time of 17 minutes and 4.2 seconds over the 15-mile course) was second in a BRM. And, before we forget, Patricia Hockley carried the title of 'Miss BAS' for this year.

Silver City Airways - 1960

The year that Miss Joyce Horton reigned as 'Miss BAS' started with January seeing reports of negotiations between Eon Mekie, chairman of Silver City and Sir Brian Robertson, from the British Transport Commission, on the possibility of future joint developments of rail-air services linking Britain with the Continent. These discussions had been conducted for some time before the news was leaked, but were vetoed by the Government in March when they announced they felt it was unwise for the BTC to consider acquiring a reported £3M minority shareholding in Silver City under the present circumstances.

This decision though was clouded in mystery, first because the BTC would not give a reason for refusing the link-up (although in principle they were sympathetic to the proposal), and secondly because Sir Brian was understood to have been willing to invest heavily in the airline. Also, while the Ministry had warned railway chiefs that within five years BEA (who were proposing to use the penny-a-mile, 110-seat, Vickers Vanguard prop-jet) and other airlines would be skimming the cream off the long-distance passenger business, there was generally believed to be two other reasons pertaining to the rejection. First the bad state of railway finances, and secondly Silver City's proposed plans to buy new vehicle-ferry aircraft and spares to the value of £4M. This latter consideration, with Silver City as ever far from a stable financial situation, was only expected to put a further burden on BTC resources.

However, whilst the BTC was precluded under its constitution from directly operating air services, it was nevertheless empowered to collaborate with an airline if it so chose, and in this capacity had already co-operated with Silver City and the French railways in running the low-fare 'Silver Arrow' service. As for Silver City, they were looking forward to a closer collaboration with British Railways mainly due to the advantages this could bring in the development of UK internal rail-air services, whilst bearing in mind such ideas as train services to points well away from built-up areas from which passengers would be brought to their aircraft. They could then be flown to destinations closer to other cities from where the journey could be completed by train.

Further underlining the Governments' decision was the impending question mark over the proposals for a tunnel (or bridge) link across the English Channel, the report on which was to be published later in the year by the Channel Tunnel Study Group. There was also another Planning Board set up to advise the Government on the various details of the envisaged rail reorganisation, this Board including representatives of the Government and the BTC as well as industrialists experienced in large undertakings. Prospective traffic development was also to come from within the sphere of its advices, and until the Board had finished its findings the Government had a legitimate excuse for their silence, as had Silver City and the BTC as well, who also refused to comment on the Government directive.

Whether or not it was ever honestly believed that negotiations would be re-opened after the Boards' findings, 20 April finally saw the publication of the Study Group report on the Channel Tunnel, the revelations of which were to promote an immediate reaction from Mr Mekie decrying the proposal of either tunnel or bridge as 'commercial folly'. For their part however the Study Group reasoned that (at that time) a tunnel was more cost-agreeable to the £200M it was estimated would be required for a bridge (the first proposal for a tunnel was made to Napoleon in 1802 when he was considering invading England, others occurred at various times between 1867 and 1957. See article in 'The Sphere' of 18 June 1960).

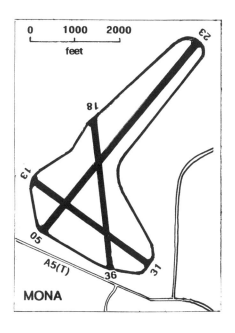

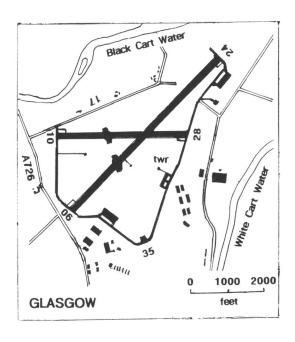

As the conclusion to a 2½-year investigation the Groups' report intimated that it could be built by 1965 at an estimated cost of around £109M, including some £500,000 of proposals for a road tunnel, railway tunnel, an immersed tube and a bridge. It concluded that a 35 minute, 32 mile long 'undersea' tunnel or tube link could be best approached if the first stage carried a railway rather than a road, due to its early earning capacity. A tunnel carrying a roadway alone would involve some problems with ventilation, the possibility of breakdowns, the strain on drivers going in excess of 20 miles in a tunnel, and also cost £129M - £152M. The arguement put forward was that if a road tunnel went into service by 1965 its capacity would have to be doubled by 1980. At this time a rail tunnel would have the capacity to absorb 70% more than the estimated peak traffic – a calculation based on 110 trains per day in each direction, up to a theoretical capacity of 216 trains, this all being based on results of surveys carried out in July, August and October 1958 on some 56,044 cross-Channel passengers to ascertain the pattern of trade to the Continent.

One stipulation was that the proposed railway station terminals should be between Ashford and Folkestone, and near Calais in France, and were expected to be around 44 miles apart. The earning power was visualised at £13M gross in 1965 and £21M in 1980, and assumed that a substantial diversion of traffic away from seaborne and air services was realised.

For his part Mr Mekie drew up a number of points opposing the project. These were principally :-

1) Technological advantages in transport generally (and aviation especially) were so rapid that it was no longer possible to foresee, for even ten years ahead, the type, speed or method of propulsion of a vehicle in which one would travel,
2) It was conceivable that within 20 years or less (perhaps before even a bridge or tunnel could be completed) cars, lorries, ships and even trains would not have wheels, but would operate on the hovercraft principle,
3) The cost of freight transportation by rail or road was, generally speaking, much more than by sea,
4) Car traffic crossing the English Channel between October and April was minimal,
5) Neither a tunnel nor bridge could provide the quick, personal service currently available to air ferry passengers, and
6) Any major structural failure or act of terrorist sabotage (or a fire?) occurring to either a tunnel or bridge would almost completely sever everyday communication between Britain and the Continent.

In summing up the attitude of Silver City's Mr Mekie stated that it was quite unthinkable for anyone to spend in excess of £100M to produce a feat of engineering which would then be rendered obsolete by the speed of modern technological advances. But indeed the most intriguing comment was made in probably the shortest letter ever sent to The Times, and published on 26 July 1960, when he wrote of the argument on cross-Channel transport under the heading 'Tunnel or Bridge', just two words – 'why either'.

However, and without going into the complete arguments for and against all the schemes which (apart from their fantastic expense) ranged between what has already been mentioned to large size 200-seat hydrofoils or an equally big hovercraft, in the construction of either a tunnel or bridge there would have been prodigious maintenance costs. What was possibly more topical regarding a bridge was the unprintable idioms spoken by certain seamen, to quote one article written for the 'Shipbuilding and Shipping Record', who thought that 'the stage would indeed be reached when the English Channel became a boatway and the pilots would be thicker than pilchards at Looe'.

Finally the decision was left firmly and squarely in the lap of Parliament, where there still echoed the annoyance of military types who in 1881 had strongly argued against the breaching of our natural defence by a tunnel – and having had visions of hoards of enemy soldiers en route to London after breakfast in France and elevenses in Kent – it was finally decided to cool the project until monetry considerations could be ascertained. This was even after it was suggested the project might be given to private investors who would be prepared to find most of the capital. For an enterprise costing some £130M, it was also suggested that the nationalised railway systems might provide £30M, and of the remaining £100M some 50% could be found from ordinary risk capital with the rest in fixed interest bonds.

As to Silver City's vehicle ferry services in 1960, in January it was announced that the Lydd to Ostend service would originate from Manston, thereby clipping ten minutes off the route time. On this new 25-minute service, approved by the MTCA for operation from 1 April up to 31 March 1967, the company also announced cuts in the summer rates for both vehicles and passengers by which passenger fares reduced by 6s after 1 April and car rates went down from 10s to £3-10s (according to length) on 16 June. This service was restarted from Lydd as from 1 December due to pressure on the Manston facilities brought about by military trooping (3 October saw SCA start an airlift for the Air Ministry, using the 70-seater Hermes to carry about 3,500 servicemen and their families monthly between Manston and Wildenrath and Dusseldorf) and other passenger commitments there, even though a new passenger terminal had been opened to serve both the Ostend vehicle ferry service and the 'Silver Arrow' operation.

Generally speaking though, low off-peak fares from Lydd were applicable on all but their summer Deauville service (which was resumed on 1 June 1960 for a limited period) and applied up to the middle of June instead of ending on 31 May. In addition, the number of days on which peak fares applied between Britain and the Continent was reduced from 20 days in each direction to 16 days outward and 12 days on return flights. However service frequencies were increased to a maximum of 300 cross-Channel flights a day instead of the 250 as scheduled in the summer of 1959.

For the 'Silver Arrow' operation, from 25 June this was stepped up to two services a day in either direction which left London at 0840 and 1440, and Paris at 0845 and 1421 hrs. From 29 May the return fare was £9-9s compared with the carried-through 1959 rate of £8-19s, and for passengers joining the service at Margate the coach fare to Manston was just 2s-6d. With regard to the 'relief' services leaving London at 1440 and Paris at 1421 hrs, the outward journey took an extra 40 minutes and the return 22 minutes longer, this being due to no special train service having been provided by the SNCF, passengers being carried on a scheduled boat express which made a special stop at Etaples to pick up and set down.

At this juncture it is interesting to compare the other options available to those intending to travel between London and Paris. Back in September 1955 Skyways utilised the then recently re-opened Lympne Airport for a new coach-air service between Victoria Coach Station and Beauvais Airport, then linked to a coach connection for Paris. This ran using East Kent Road Car Company luxury coaches to Lympne, Dakotas on the one-hour air crossing to France and luxury coaches of Transports Renaults for the journey into the heart of Paris. In 1955 the average journey time on this route, including check-in, was six hours 50 minutes, and with a return fare on Mondays to Thursdays of £7-14s (rising to £8-15s at weekends) 44lbs of baggage was allowed to carried free. Passengers joining at Lympne only paid £6-4s-6d return plus 15s for the coach journey between Beauvais and Paris. With Skyways Coach-Air operation still being the best option service between both capitals in 1960, the other main alternatives were as follows:-

	Return fare (a)	Average time (including check-in)
Cheapest rail-sea (Newhaven-Dieppe)	£8-9s	8hrs 45mins
Skyways Coach-Air (off-peak flights)	£8-10s (b)	5hrs 50mins
Silver Arrow (rail-air)	£9-9s	6hrs 45mins
IATA airlines (night tourist)	£11-12s-6d	3hrs 25mins

(a) these return fares covered transport but not meals. The IATA rates included airport taxes and coach fares
(b) Skyways also operated special night tourist flights with even cheaper rates.

On 15 June, with the development of this route in mind, Silver City then extended their no-passport excursions to Paris introduced in 1959 with a new 48-hour, two-way no-passport trip to the capital for both British and French nationals. This service, operated by Inter City Tours using Dakotas from either Lydd or Manston at 0900 hrs on Tuesdays and Wednesdays via Le Touquet, was designed to appeal to to visitors wanting to spend an inexpensive two days in either capital. Fares for the service, which originated from Victoria Coach Station, including two nights in a second class hotel in Paris, was £11-11s or £9-9s, according to whether a train or coach was used in France. For those joining the service at the airport the rate was £11 or £8-18s respectively. An additional weekend trip was later arranged which departed from either Lydd or Manston at 0730 hrs on Saturdays to arrive back late on Sunday evening, the fare being £7-7s for this shorter excursion.

In June Silver City's associate company, Manx Airlines, also applied for ATAC permission to run a vehicle ferry service between Squires Gate airport, Blackpool, and Ronaldsway Airport, Isle of Man for a period of seven years using Freighters. Nothing however seems to have come from this application, possibly due to the implications of a Dan-Air intention to run a similar service between Liverpool, Blackpool and Valley to the Isle of Man.

As to Silver City's northern passenger division during 1960, Newcastle was replaced by Blackpool as the starting point for the Leeds/Bradford to Brussels service, a route stopped two years previous due to few people using the service. Blackpool was again added to the Newcastle to Amsterdam and Dusseldorf services. From 1 June to September the flights left Blackpool at 0915 on Mondays and Thursdays, arriving at Leeds/Bradford at 0945 and Brussels at at 1300 hrs. For the other Blackpool service the flight left at 0830 to arrive in Newcastle at 1000, Amsterdam at 1300 and Dusseldorf at 1415 hrs. This service began with two flights a week from 1 April and increased frequency from 4 May to 28 September to three flights on Mondays, Wednesdays and Fridays (eventually it was carried through to 1 November, then to March 1961 at a frequency of two flights a week, after which it resumed at the summer frequency). The northern division were still continuing to operate their usual services to the Isle of Man from Blackpool, Glasgow, Newcastle, Edinburgh, Birmingham, Leeds/Bradford and Carlisle. Other routes were Newcastle and Blackpool to Leeds/Bradford, Leeds/Bradford to Jersey, and Blackpool to Belfast and Dublin.

Other company activities during the year included the carriage of 100 Austin Seven cars to Le Touquet in February for the British Motor Corporation, after the ending of import restrictions on British cars coincided with an increased demand for the new model (exactly one year later SCA was involved in flying a quantity of Renault Estavette vans from Le Touquet to Lydd). Other charters in the news included those for the carriage of oysters, regular shipments of the 'Radio Times', and a particularly notable one was for four tons of furnishings and fittings flown to the Isle of Man for a lounge bar to be installed in the Golf

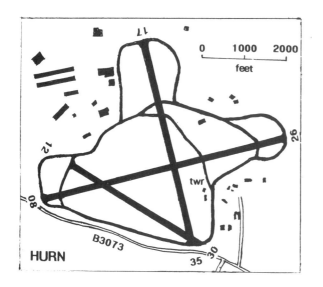

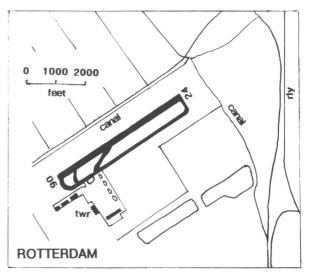

Links Hotel at Castletown. On the lighter side, however, in June a new amenity was provided at Lydd for travellers to occupy their waiting-for-takeoff-time – a zoo. This amusement, reportedly the first ever of its type at a British airport for both passengers and visitors, was provided by the Chipperfield circus family and included a bear, kangaroo, llamas, golden pheasants and chimpanzees, and it was stated categorically by SCA that none of the animals would, at any time, be allowed anywhere near the aircraft. At various times other types of 'entertainment' for waiting passengers were tried, including the 'self-drive' 'Crested Wren' hovercraft, a track for which was sited next to the Air Kruise building in 1968.

1960 also saw a number of anniversaries celebrated, the first of these in June when, to commemorate the fiftieth anniversary of the two-way crossing of the Channel by the Hon C S Rolls on 2 June 1910, the twelfth of Silver City's own vehicle ferry operation, and the official rebirth of Le Touquet (Paris Plage) airport after its destruction by the RAF on 13 June 1944, Silver City held a reception at the Westminster Hotel, Le Touquet. Then as a way of re-enacting the first balloon crossing of the English Channel by the Frenchman Jean Pierre Blanchard in 1785, Koen Jansen, a 33 year-old Dutchman, and his co-pilot Alex Valentine, took off from Ferryfield at 1239 on 2 September to cross the Channel using a hydrogen-filled envelope. This was reported as the first cross-Channel balloon flight since 1913, however the balloon drifted 100 miles off course and finally landed at Oostkamp, a town six miles from Brussels, instead of Calais as planned.

Nevertheless, and in a year which was to see Silver City aircraft flying from Hurn during August with food for the strikebound Channel Islands, as with previous years the company kept up the trend of further developments. In October they again expanded their 'Roadair' service by introducing a new twice-weekly service between their Chelsea Bridge depot and Holland, similar to the existing service to Belgium. Prior to this in September they had introduced a road link between the Chelsea Bridge depot and Hurn in connection with the existing 'Roadair' service between Hurn and Jersey. Later in the year they also secured a five year contract for the checking of radio aids on overseas bases including Cyprus, Bahrain, Shanah, Lagos, Kano (Nigeria) and Accra (Ghana).

In December Silver City then announced more fare reductions for the coming 1961 season, which followed the pattern for previous years and applied to all the vehicle ferry services from Lydd and Hurn and, if applicable, Manston. Primarily in an effort to extend yet again the summer seasons off-peak fares they upheld these for the 40 weeks of operations from Tuesday 19 September to Friday 20 June, instead of the 36 weeks in the 1960 season. This was claimed to be the longest period of off-peak fares ever operated by any cross-Channel ferry operator, either by sea or air. Peak fares were still levied during the three busiest summer months but the surcharge applicable to weekends from July to September was dispensed with – which amounted to something like a £4 saving on the transportation of an average length car. Thus with this concession the company only ran two basic levels of fare – an off-peak level applicable for over ¾ of the year and a higher level for the rest of the time. Along with this, a startling reduction was applied to the rate for motorcycles and scooters under 250cc, their rates were cut from £1 to 2s-6d – the same price charged for bicycles. A company stipulation at this time was that the maximum vehicle height allowed on their ferries was 6'-6", but for 1961 this limit was raised to 6'-10" when it was found that even larger vehicles only rose slightly on their springs once they were in the hold and shackled down. This small change thus opened up the market to many more car users.

Silver City's statistics for 1960 showed that, in January alone, Ferryfield handled 3240 passengers, 5127 short tons of freight and experienced 1681 aircraft movements, compared with 2676, 2108 and 613 respectively in 1959. In the six months leading up to 5 April the company flew 10,740 British and foreign export cars across the Channel compared with 5852 in the whole 12 months ending 30 September 1959. The total carried for the twelve months ending 30 September 1960 was 90,332 vehicles and almost 220,000 passengers and accompanying cars in 40,000 Channel crossings. The total for freight also jumped up, to a record 135,607 tons, an increase of 35% over 1959 figures – probably a world record for any airline in 1960. For the vehicle ferries the most impressive car traffic increases were recorded on the Manston to Ostende and Hurn to Cherbourg services. The Ostende route handled double the traffic experienced at Lydd during 1959, while on the Cherbourg route the total cars ferried was in excess of 10,000, compared with 7400 in 1959.

In October 1960, with their previous experience of the outcome of applications for 'deep penetration' routes, but already holding a licence to operate between Birmingham and Le Touquet, Silver City then applied for permission to develop five new vehicle ferry services between the North of England, Scotland, and Frances' northern coast for a seven year period commencing on 1 March 1961. On these services, initially using Freighters but later on the Breguet 763 to carry vehicles and passengers, and incidental passengers and supplemental freight at an initial frequency of six return flights a day on each sector, the routes were –

Le Touquet and/or Calais and/or Cherbourg to –
1) Leeds/Bradford
2) Blackpool and/or Liverpool and/or Manchester
3) Glasgow and/or Edinburgh
4) Newcastle, and
Newcastle to Amsterdam.

At this time the company also applied to carry incidental passengers and supplementary freight 'without restriction' on their already-authorised vehicle ferry services between Lydd or Manston and,

1) Cologne, at a frequency of two return flights a day
2) Le Touquet (optional) and Pontoise, at a frequency of six return flights a day
3) Le Touquet (optional) and Troyes, at a frequency of three return flights a day.

The consequence of these applications was seen in February 1961, when reports were first published of the proposed amalgamation of company interests with Cie Air Transport. This link which had, from the outset, stemmed from Silver City's past association with CAT, in reality came from their proposal to develop services between the provincial centres of Britain and the French coast, and the fact that they had failed to secure a deal with the BTC. Since then they had been looking for another route on which to obtain re-equipment capital – hence the political significance of the inclusion of the Breguet 763 in the service application.

In retrospect though, CAT was obviously a worthwhile route by which they might achieve their objective. Not only had the companies worked with one another in the past, but CAT's principle shareholder was the French State Railways (SNCF) which had, for the past four years, been an essentially non-operating partner on Silver City's London to Paris 'Silver Arrow' service. Silver City therefore appreciated that, if CAT were actively involved in their expansion programme, this co-operation could lead to an integrated air-rail and vehicle ferry operation into the heart of France. A decision such as this would also, they hoped, pave the way for their much-needed replacement aircraft.

With the foregoing in mind during negotiations with both CAT and SNCF, it was agreed that, to enable CAT to fully integrate with the British operation, Silver City would transfer three of their Freighter Mk 32s over to CAT to be used in their French livery on the vehicle ferry routes from Le Touquet and Calais to Lydd, and Cherbourg to Hurn, and it was even mooted to run between Calais and Southend (records at Companies House show that the three aircraft were sold to CAT, and that CAT director Jacques Ottensooser also became a director of SCA on 21 March). In return SNCF agreed to build a two-mile rail spur to connect Etaples railway station with Le Touquet airport (proposed in 1959), this being due for completion by the summer of 1962.

The significance of this link was that passenger services would assume a much greater part of the prospective traffic, and with Silver City's proposed internal network of air services passengers would be able to fly direct to Calais and Cherbourg – and especially Le Touquet – from where they would be able to continue their journey by train to any point on the

Ten years after G-AHJO was used by SCA it was back with them in 1959 when on loan from British Eagle, in whose colours (but with SCA titling) it is seen at Lydd on 15 July, framed by the Bleriot replica F-PERV which was taking part in the Dail Mail London to Paris air race (photo by Ken Honey).

Publicity shot of the proposed ATL98 car-ferry replacement for the Freighter, shown in Channel Air Bridge colour scheme. Two points of note here; one that the door cill height precluded the use of 'Freighter' type ramps (the scissor-lift Hylo being used instead), secondly that the model has endplates on the tailplane for directional stability, this being one of the design options looked at by ATEL but not used (ATEL photo via Arthur Leftley).

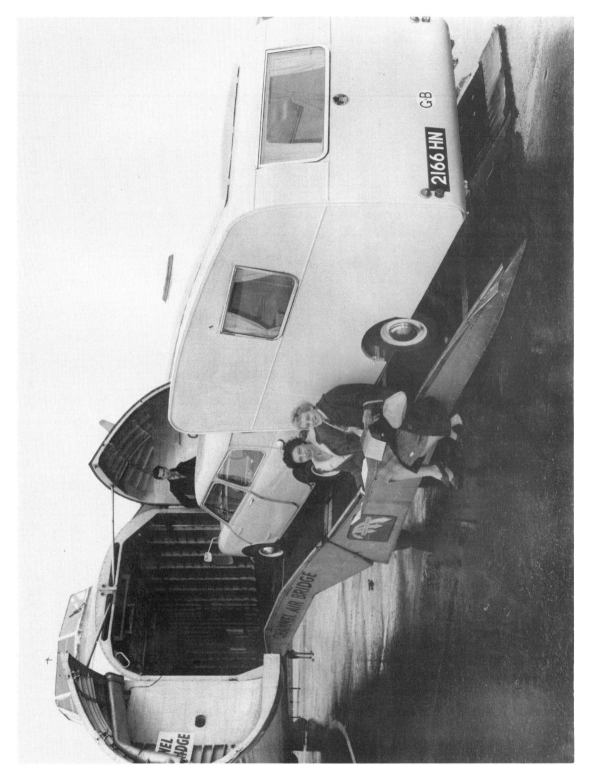

Apart from cars other vehicles carried included caravans, one of which is about to be eased (or squeezed?) into the freight hold of CAB Freighter Mk 32 G–AMLP Bridge along with its Mini towing vehicle (photo by Highlands).

DAF cars being loaded into a CAB Freighter Mk 32 at Southend for return to Rotterdam after the Motor Show at Earls Court in October 1958. This was the first small automatic car, the transmission final drive being by means of rubber belts. In the background construction of the new Aviation Traders maintenance hangar is underway, with director Bob Batt's Percival Prentice and the tail of C54B G-ANYB just evident in the shot (photo by Geroy).

SCA Freighter Mk 21 G-AIME at the Joyfield 'mobile' oil survey camp, some 250 miles south of Tripoli, on 3 February 1959. Operated by the D'Arcy Corporation of Africa on behalf of Shell-BP, one of its vehicles can be seen collecting essential supplies for loading into 'IME for onward transfer to other camps (photo by Ken Honey).

SCA Freighter Mk 21 G-AIME at the Joyfield 'mobile' oil survey camp on 3 February 1959, loading some of the more essential supplies for onward shipment to French camps in the Lybian desert, as a diversion to the normal routine of personnel and equipment transfer associated with the oil exploration work being carried out. Although on lease to Shell-BP it was working with the D'Arcy Corporation of Africa, both of whose insignia can be seen on the lorry door in both Arabic and English (photo by Ken Honey).

It was as a result of vigilance on such flights in November 1958 that Ken Honey and other crewmen located the B24 Liberator 'Lady Be Good', from the 514th Squadron, 376th Bomb Group, USAF, that force-landed in the Lybian desert when it overflew its Bengazi base in April 1943 after its first operation, a raid on Naples. Later visits by the oil companies to the desert in February-August 1960 resulted in the remains of most of the crew being found, after the extensive and organised search by the American military had produced nothing.

Continent. As to the motorist, he too would be able to start his journey on the Continent without having to drive southwards through England, alternatively if he wanted to avoid the drive through France he could arrange for his car to be taken to a point nearer to his destination from the Le Touquet railhead.

Whilst Silver City's alliance with CAT could, as far as the traveller was concerned, only serve to everybody's advantage, this amalgamation did little to boost Freighter utilisation as the type was mainly confined to the cross-Channel routes. Any development in the direction of the envisaged network of internal services would need much more time to integrate, bearing in mind the complexities of operation in terms of maximum traffic demands and aircraft utilisation. With this in mind, Silver City felt that if sufficient passengers could be attracted to the Le Touquet railhead they could delay matters relating to replacement of the Freighter until the capital outlay could be justified to their owners, the P&O group – a company who had seen a poor return from the Hermes aircraft so expensively obtained in 1954.

As mentioned earlier, although Silver City had used the Breguet 761 on trials into Berlin the type was never to be used on the vehicle ferry services. Due to the economics of their envisaged network which was more likely to depend on passenger rather than pure vehicle cartage, or at least until motorists became wealthier or developed new habits, the aircraft requirement in establishing these routes (assuming they could re-equip) would have to be of a type that would break even on passenger loads alone. In this respect the only real choice at this time, apart from the Breguet and other designs mooted in the 1959 chapters, would be re-distribution of the Freighter fleet, but this in itself was not really feasible in the light of CAT's acquisition of three Mk 32s which had, at a stroke, reduced the group's effectiveness. A major point to consider was that, with the fleet fitted out in an economical passenger configuration very similar to that of the Super Wayfarer when flown on the 'Silver Arrow' services, if vehicles were required to be flown from the North of England to France on an on-demand basis, any aircraft used would be delayed until the interiors were reconfigured for the consignment, thus causing the service to be a non-starter. Another choice would have been to use Dakotas from the Northern division for the passenger runs, and only sending a Freighter when the need arose. This alternative was also unrealistic due to all the Dakotas being fully utilised during the peak periods and the hit-and-miss idea of providing a Freighter on demand would not always be possible.

Out of all this the most obvious effect of the amalgamation was that, in reality, this joining could force Channel Air Bridge out of the French interior and off their 'deep penetration' routes to Lyons and Strasbourg. Also, in any further agreement on service applications into central France, the French government, remembering CAT's allegiance to SNCF, would be more likely to favour Silver City's applications, even though the main opponents of these routes would most likely be SNCF itself – a prediction that was to ring true in later days.

Silver City Airways – 1961

In February 1961, with the background to the amalgamation in mind, and the probability of an impending battle with Channel Air Bridge over the prospects of 'deep penetration' operations, Silver City announced the start of a new vehicle ferry service between Guernsey and Maupertus Airport, Cherbourg at a weekly frequency until 9 September and thereafter at an increased frequency. Shortly after this, and with the reluctance of British Railways to pursue the proposed railway spur into Manston, Silver City announced in March that their 'Silver Arrow' service would be operated from Lydd from 23 June to 18 September. This service had been suspended at Manston on 1 October 1960 due to the company's trooping commitments, and the schedule was revised in respect of the rail service to Margate and coach service from there to Manston which were both replaced by a coach link between London and Lydd. Hermes aircraft operated the cross-Channel service to Le Touquet, while the French side of the operation was continued as before with express diesel cars, and the return fare was also reduced from £9-9s to £8-15s (less than the 1959 rate), even though the overall journey time went down from six hours 45 minutes to six hours 25 minutes.

As to Silver City's own personnel, a report was published in April giving the circumstances by which Albert Hayes had gained his captaincy. Whilst working as a driver some eight years previous he had designed the 'shack-clip', which reduced the time it took to secure vehicles to the cargo deck of the Freighter. Instead of accepting payment for this idea, and as he had been a pilot with the RAF, he requested in return that he be trained as a pilot for the company, and in doing so completed his training as first officer in 1955.

Regarding Silver City's general activities during 1961, since the takeover of the Air Kruise inclusive tour services back in October 1957 the number of organisations, and tour and charter operators actively involved with Silver City had steadily increased. In fact, other than the two or three already mentioned, there had been quite a few; Wallace Arnold Tours Ltd, McBean Tours Ltd, Lumbs Continental Tours Ltd, Leroy Tours, Blue Cars Continental Coach Cruises Ltd and Voyagers Ltd. Indeed, in this respect the company had been no less prolific in its new applications than in previous years.

Nothwithstanding the foregoing, a black cloud overshadowed the company's new Cherbourg to Guernsey vehicle ferry service when, after a missed approach on 1 November, their Mk 32, G-ANWL, crashed at Guernsey with ten people and three cars on board. At the Board of Enquiry it was stated that, after missing his first approach, the pilot opened up both his engines to go around but the aircraft failed to gain height. Veering to the right it flew for a short distance with the starboard propellor rotating slowly before the starboard wingtip struck the ground and the aircraft cartwheeled. The passenger cabin broke away from the main wreckage, which caught fire, seven passengers and the flight crew were killed and the steward seriously injured. The accident was attributed to a loss of momentum caused by the automatic pitch-coarsening safety device to the starboard propellor having cut in at the time full power was applied, this sudden asymmetric thrust at low altitude causing the aircraft to crash. The pilot, George Hogarth, had been with SCA for many years and had, amongst other attributes, been captain on the inaugural flight of the Eastleigh to Bembridge service on 2 July 1953.

Just after this, the first fatal accident on 250,397 vehicle ferry flights, the Company also had further problems. On applying to the ATLB for permission to operate three incidental passenger services, the applications were rejected, due to (so it was said) SCA's reluctance to invest in new aircraft. Although there were many who disagreed strongly with the views held by a 'licensing board', the official reasons behind the refusals were:-

SCA application	Reason for refusal
Lydd/Manston to Basle	BUA favoured
Manston/Hurn/London to Marseilles and Genoa	BEA & BUA favoured
Manston/Hurn/London to Lisbon and Madeira	BUA favoured.

These latter developments, and the ATLB's unexpected change of heart towards Silver City, had most probably resulted from news in November of the company's impending merger with the British United Airways group of companies (BUA), which had been widely awaited for some time. For this amalgamation (detailed elsewhere) a new company with the name of Air Holdings Ltd was formed, exclusively by British United shareholders, and in which the shareholders of BAS were invited to participate (to a reported 20% interest). Having its initial registered capital of £100 increased to a nominal £600,000, Air Holdings then made an offer to acquire, on the basis of exchange stock, the entire shareholdings in both BUA and BAS. This offer was accepted by all the shareholders.

For Silver City this takeover could not have been more distasteful due to the longstanding rivalry between the company and Channel Air Bridge, BUA's subsidiary in the field of vehicle ferry operations. Now because Mr F A Laker had previously managed CAB's parent company (Air Charter), and was both executive director of BUA and a director of Air Holdings, Silver City's services which had originally set the pattern for CAB's vehicle ferry activities would now most likely be co-ordinated using the new BUA-developed ATL98 aircraft that had been test-flown in June. This was a type in which Silver City had themselves shown an interest when Michael Day, the Silver City technical director, approached Aviation Traders on the possibility of purchasing one once it was fully flight-proven.

Silver City Airways - 1962

The outcome of the merger became evident in February 1962 when it was reported that Mr Eoin C Mekie CBE, chairman of both BAS and Silver City since 1950, had resigned. Eoin Mekie, who was often described as a man of many interests, was born in Edinburgh on 3 November 1906 and in 1929 qualified fully as a solicitor after passing through Watson's, Edinburgh University. Moving to London in 1935, he was for 13 years director of fifteen different electrical companies before changing careers at 42, after the industry had been nationalised, to become Silver City chairman two years later. Along with Air Commodore Powell he was largely responsible for the company's earlier achievements, and in 1955 he received a CBE for his 'political and public services in Woodmanston', having previously stood for Parliament as Leith's prospective Unionist candidate in 1950 and 1951. In 1956 he was director of some 25 companies and chairman of ten others while in 1960, as well as his political and airline committments, he held 30 directorships ranging from insurance and banking to cement and chipboard companies.

Mr Mekie's resignation was also accompanied by those of other BAS Board members. These were:- Sir Donald Anderson, chairman of P & O and now director of Air Holdings, Mr A J M M Crichton, managing director of P & O, Mr R G Grout, director of P & O and chairman of their subsidiary, the G S & N Co, General Sir Edwin Morris, director of Eagle Star Insurance, and Sir Arthur Vere Harvey. Mr Laker, on the other hand, joined the board of Silver City as its deputy chairman with effect from 7 February 1962 (until his subsequent resignation on 25 November 1965).

After this the next news with any direct bearing on Silver City's own employees occurred in March when a decision by Air Holdings to strengthen their operation involved moving all the latters personnel at Manston to Gatwick. This, a spokesman said, would result in substantial operating economies and be of benefit to the group as a whole.

It was thus with speculation of an impending integration of the Silver City and Channel Air Bridge vehicle ferrying activities, possibly under a new name, that it was announced on 25 July that both companies ferry divisions would henceforth trade under the name of British United Air Ferries, with Silver City's scheduled and inclusive tour services being integrated into the group by the summer of 1962. The chairman of the new ferry organisation was Mr Miles Wyatt (chairman of Air Holdings and BUA), with Freddie Laker as its managing director and Douglas Wybrow its general manager. Miles Wyatt also joined Freddie Laker on the board of Silver City.

The transition period, which was expected to run to the end of 1962, eventually resulted in the actual amalgamation of the two companies services taking place on 1 January 1963, but even after this date some of the aircraft still carried their individual names.

Again Silver City's operations since September 1960 had again been impressive. In the twelve months to 30 September 1961, they had carried some 87,466 cars (of which 4346 were for export) and 225,156 passengers in a total of 38,341 Channel crossings. Also in the twelve months to 31 March 1962 Silver City, and their associate company CAT, carried 96,272 cars (including 16,888 for export) and 238,748 passengers in 43,064 Channel crossings. For the period between 1 December 1961 and 30 November 1962, the combined BUAF traffic for both Silver City (with CAT) and Channel Air Bridge on their vehicle ferry routes reached a figure of 137,730 cars, 4182 motorcycles, 425,333 passengers and 22,800 tons of cargo. In all the Freighters also made 63,200 Channel crossings representing some 34,700 passenger miles, 11,300,000 car miles and 19,000,000 revenue ton miles. On their integral passenger services in parallel with the vehicle ferry routes they had also carried an additional 138,380 passengers in 3680 Channel crossings, symbolising 12,200,000 passenger miles and 11,000,000 revenue miles.

The final consequences of the amalgamation were realised in November 1962 when, with the ATLB's attitude still pertaining, the following Silver City vehicle ferry route applications were revoked, thus sealing once and for all the company's fate-

1) Newcastle to Le Touquet and/or Calais and/or Cherbourg,
2) Lydd or Manston to Le Touquet (optional) to Troyes, and
3) Lydd or Manston to Le Touquet (optional) to Pentoise.

Additionally the following licences were suspended –

1) Leeds/Bradford to Le Touquet and/or Calais and/or Cherbourg,
2) Blackpool and/or Manchester and/or Liverpool to Le Touquet and/or Calais and/or Cherbourg,
3) Bournemouth or London (Gatwick) or Lydd to Deauville or Le Havre, and
4) Newcastle to Amsterdam (between 26 October 1962 and 4 April 1963).

With this, and the events of early 1963, Silver City Airways, as far as the general public was concerned, ceased to exist, although even at the time of writing (1975), the company name was still used in connection with some activities at Lydd and the general freighting and overhaul services appertaining to that airport. CAT still exists as a freighting agency, but as far as vehicle ferry services were concerned their involvement was greatly reduced until it finally ceased in the early 1970's. The vehicle ferry operation was considered by all who worked on it to be 'the good old days', people worked hard (and generally ran around everywhere), the summer season was the busiest, with an aircraft landing, another taking off, one taxying out, and others being loaded, the sort of activity that will never be repeated.

Aviation Traders

While the activities of Silver City Airways and its associate companies stood out among their contemporaries, it was true to say that the beginnings of Air Charter were more in keeping with the majority of British independants. The company, which became operational in 1952 was then owned by Mr F A Laker who in 1947 had ventured into aeronautical engineering following his return to civil life in 1946.

Born in Canterbury on 6 August 1922 Freddie Laker's career in aviation started as an apprentice at Shorts, Rochester, and had been inspired, he has stated, by his sighting of the German airship 'Hindenburg' together with a Handley Page HP42 of Imperial Airways flying in the sky over Canterbury. However, even if the will was there the way was not, because with the outbreak of the Second World War he joined the Air Transport Auxiliary to ferry aircraft for the RAF, not as a pilot but a flight engineer, one of his jobs being to compile the necessary 'Pilots Notes' for each type. Demobbed in 1946 with a gratuity of just £40 he became a door-to-door salesman selling seedlings before joining (as a flight engineer) the newly-formed London Aero Motor Services with its subsidiary companies in South Africa and Australia. When the downfall of LAMS came he decided he could make more money on his own (as his part-time dabbling in second-hand cars had shown) and moved into the surplus aircraft business to found, along with others, Aviation Traders Ltd.

Being completely non-operational, Aviation Traders Ltd was registered on 17 October 1947 with a capital of £100 in 100 £1 shares, and was described as 'being able to carry on the business of merchants and distributors of, and agents for dealers in, aircraft and aircraft parts, spares and equipment etc', and had but two subscribers with one share each – Mr Albert E Careless and Mr Kenneth J Bateman. The two registered directors were Mr F A Laker and Mr Alfred L Hughes.

In trading from their base at Bovingdon, Hertfordshire in 1948, and having just helped a Scottish friend, Bobby Sanderson, dispose of some aircraft, Laker was asked if the favour could be returned. Over drinks in the Silver Cross public house in Whitehall Laker could visualise the possibilities of purchasing BOAC's entire fleet of twelve Halton transports that had just come onto the market and intimated that he would buy these aircraft if he had the money. The result was that Sanderson loaned him £38,000 to add to his own £4,000 and he did just that, also acquiring 600 tons of spare parts in the process, and after a deal had been settled with Bond Aircraft Services, who also operated the type in Germany, six of the Haltons were flown around the clock on the Berlin Airlift. The remaining six were sold and parts from the vast spares mountain used to keep those in service operational.

Realising the need to have his own aircraft overhaul and repair facilities Laker then formed an associate company with the name of Aviation Traders (Engineering) Ltd which was duly registered on 8 March 1949. Specialising initially in the repair of aircraft supplied by the founder company AT(E)L (as it became known) was based at its newly-acquired premises at the municipal airport at Southend, Essex, and complemented the vast store of British and American aircraft parts that Aviation Traders had built up at Bovingdon by supplying the necessary expertise to overhaul a number of Handley Page Halifax aircraft that had been bought up in a drive to corner that particular market. In this respect, and by buying up all the then available Halifax spares, the company was thus equipped to offer a unique service to all Halifax operators, whether military or civil, an activity which was undertaken with Handley Page's full authority.

Some of these early acquisitions included ex-RAF B Mk 6 bombers, C Mk 8 transports and the A Mk 9 Airbourne transports, and AT(E)L was indeed fortunate in being called on to re-equip the Royal Egyptian Air Force with a number of the A Mk 9 versions. For this contract, the work on which was started in November 1949 and the first Halifax delivered via Malta the following January, the aircraft were brought up to full military standard with an armament of one Vickers gun in the nose and two Browning machine guns in the tail turret, together with provision for bombs or supply canisters in the bomb bay. Some were fitted with dual controls, while others had a freight pannier fitted in the bomb bay, but all had full radio and radar equipment fitted.

In the case of these early commitments AT(E)L soon gained full ARB approval for all their own overhaul departments, which included a plug overhaul shop fitted out completely with Lodge overhaul and test equipment. They also had a fully equipped ARB-approved radio and radar overhaul and repair section. Engine and airscrew testing was usually done in the airframe, rather than in a special engine test stand, since the Halifaxes normally had the engines already installed.

After work was complete the aircraft were flight tested and, once the C of A was issued, with the facilities afforded by Southend being a Customs Airport the complicated Customs procedure necessary to clear what were in fact fully-armed bombers was simplified before delivery was undertaken. During the same period AT(E)L also overhauled three ex-BEA Vikings for BOAC, to be used by British West Indies Airways.

As to Aviation Traders engineering department at Stansted, late in 1952 they were engaged in sub-contract production of components and spares for various aircraft manufacturers. The majority of this work was for the Bristol Aeroplane Company and involved fabricating complete wing centre sections for Bristol Type 170 Freighters and rudders for the Brigand, using jigs provided by BAC. The Type 170 wing work was deemed necessary after Bristols confirmed that both the front and rear lower spar booms had a service life of 9,000 and 10,000 landings respectively, and was a major rebuild in part which increased the number possible to 59,000. With boom repairs only allowed to be done twice landings could only be increased to 28,000, after which the aircraft was no longer airworthy, thus the need for boom and skin replacements. Other work involved the construction of doors for the Fairey Gannet, supplying spares for the Supermarine Spitfire, and machining parts for use in sub-assemblies made by Blackburn.

This entry into the engineering field represented a useful addition to their potential and was regarded by the company as the first step towards design and manufacture of a complete aircraft. For this reason a design office was built up to enable preliminary work to be carried out in this field.

Other projects were undertaken, the most interesting being their private development work on pre-stressed 'tension' skin – a double curvature with no presswork – which they hoped would be used on their proposed twin-engined turbo-prop aircraft, the ATL90.

Regarding Aviation Traders work in 1955, besides their continuing overhaul and minor engineering contracts, and with the aim of using the Air Charter Tudors more effectively, they designed and engineered at Southend a modified version of the Tudor Mk 4 designated the 'Super Trader', having double freight doors forming a freight hatch measuring 6'-10" in width and 5'-5" high on the portside fuselage, forward of the passenger door. Installation of this opening produced no major problems beyond those associated with strengthening both the fuselage around the cutout and the door to receive the freight, and involved the building up of two existing fuselage frames fore and aft of the opening, provision of beams above and below the opening between these frames, and an inner fuselage skin fitted locally around the door to carry the loads.

The prototype, G-AHNI, was test-flown at Stansted during April 1955 in passenger/freight configuration with removable seats, and followed by three further conversions, however these three, G-AHNL, 'HNM and 'HNO, differed from the prototype in that they had all-freight interiors. These aircraft then formed the backbone of Air Charter's Tudor fleet which in reality was an amalgamation of all those registered to Fairflight and Aviation Traders by all but three of the last remaining Tudors, although they had rights on these Mk 5s as well (see Appendix 10).

The 'Accountant' Saga

While Aviation Traders were converting the Tudor to a freight configuration the design and production work was ongoing at Southend on their twin-engined, turbo-prop aircraft, the ATL90. Known as the 'Accountant' this 40-seat capacity design would, it was hoped, form the basis of a much-needed Dakota replacement, and by November 1955 was well enough advanced for the company's chief designer, Mr L C Heal AFRAeS, to inform the aviation press that 'its equipment had been tested and the aircraft would probably be test-flown by the following summer'.

However, when the aircraft was eventually test-flown on 9 July 1957, one year later than expected, it had in reality only 28 seats. This change in passenger capacity had resulted after a number of revisions had followed the initial design, the most complex of which was the introduction of a forward nose cargo door whilst another, the proposal for hinging the complete nose, was finally abandoned in favour of a baggage loading door 4'-5" x 3'-7" situated on the port side behind the pilots cockpit. Also the prototype fuselage, not equipped to be pressurised and built on the tension-skin method of construction pioneered by the company, had caused problems including delays in tooling. It was therefore decided that subsequent aircraft would be built using conventional skinning methods that would eliminate the time and manpower-absorbing development needed to perfect Aviation Traders own skin construction system. This in itself had been made dubious by their own studies of more flexible methods which gave no expected weight penalties.

Nevertheless, if the said delays over the complications in the design implied that Aviation Traders were in some doubt as to the approach on how to build the 'Accountant' nothing could be further from the truth. In the first place, while the 40-seat version would have formed a sound basis for a middle-distance passenger aircraft, it was more feasible to have a version with only 28 seats (or less) which could be more adaptable as a freighter or a combined passenger freighter. This, it was felt, would be more appealing to operators who were not expected to expand their fleets in a few years to a position where more than 22 seats were required in order to obtain a break even load factor. There were operators who, while expanding at the time, still used 14 or 16-seat aircraft, and for these the 'Accountant' was designed to enable a high utilisation while its operation and maintenance was simplified by the easily accessible systems.

To this end Aviation Traders experienced design team, which had been recruited from a number of major companies, had been forward enough to settle for a Dart installation at a time when there was no accumulative operating data for this type of powerplant, and its acceptance by engineers was not so universal as was the case by 1957. Additionally, the design incorporated visually unorthodox features in respect of the high setting of the nacelle units for the Rolls Royce Darts and a correspondingly high tailplane. These both allowed a modest increase in thrust from the straight jet pipe to be utilised while not affecting the aircraft's stability – a feature which had some drawbacks during the design phase. This ultimately allowed the powerplant mountings and wing assemblies to be as straightforward as possible, thus simplifying engine replacement. The aircraft's visually humped fuselage, which for the time was somewhat unusual, was to be straightened out on subsequent aircraft.

After the test flights on 9 July 1957 as G-41-1 (the ATEL Class B marks) the aircraft was registered as G-ATEL on 30 August, and displayed at that summers' Farnborough Air Show, but misfortune befell ATEL by the end of the year. News broke first as a rumour, and then fact, which was confirmed on 10 January 1958 after 70 hours of test flying ceased following a Government decision to refuse any financial aid for further development. The aircraft was stored at Southend until May 1959 when, after ATEL's amalgamation with Airwork, Laker ordered it to be broken up and it was taken off the British register on 8 October 1959.

Indeed the disappointment which followed was even harder to take by the workforce when soon afterwards a similar aircraft by a different company appeared on the scene with an almost identical flight deck and other leading attributes. With the Avro 748 there was even talk of industrial espionage, indeed after all this had died down Traders future looked a little uncertain until the staff re-grouped to form a new design team for the ATL98 project.

Leading particulars of the 'Accountant' were:-

Dimensions	Span	82'-6"
	Length	62'-1"
	Height	25'-3½"
Wing	Area	632 sq ft
	Aspect ratio	10.77
Fuselage	Total capacity	1,670 cu ft
Powerplant	2 Rolls Royce Dart RDa 6 of 1730 ehp at take-off	
Weights	Gross	28,500 lbs
	Initial max landing	27,100 lbs
	MZFW	26,500 lbs
Performance	Max VFR stage length	2,420 st miles
	Max VMC stage with 28 passengers and luggage	1,020 st miles
	Operating altitude	25,000 ft
	Mean cruising speed	295 mph
	Stalling speed	69 kts
	Sea level balanced field length at 25,800 ft ISA	3,220 ft
	At ISA plus 15°C	3,400 ft
	At sea level and 5,000' altitude	4,000 ft
	Rate of climb SL and LSA	1,500 ft/min
	single engine	500 ft/min
	Time to 25,000 ft (both engines operating)	27.6 mins.

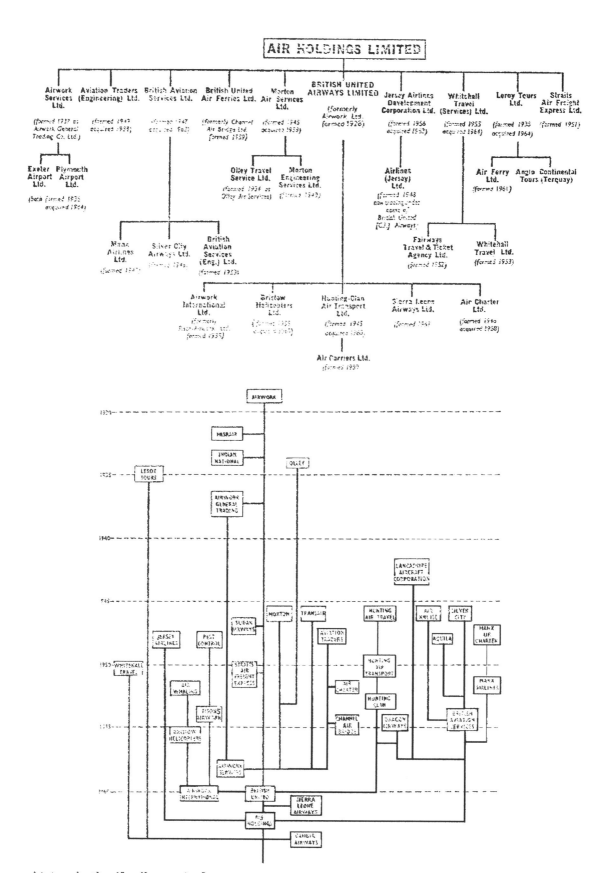

At top is the 'family tree' of company acquisition within the Air Holdings network and, below, the route from Airwork to Air Holdings. Both reproduced from *The Aeroplane and Commercial Aviation News – Air Holdings supplement* of 21 January 1965.

Fairflight Ltd

At the same time as Aviation Traders was establishing itself another company, Airflight Ltd, had also emerged. Airflight was founded by its managing director Air Vice Marshal Donald Clifford Tyndall Bennett of 'Pathfinder' fame with his wife Elsa as co-director and, registered on 4 June 1948, began operations with two Avro Tudors (a Mk 2 and Mk 5) for a short period of time on the little Berlin Airlift, before its activities were superseded by Fairflight Ltd, as a change of company name.

Fairflight Ltd was registered on 25 August 1949 with the usual minimum capital of £100 in 100 £1 shares and described to be in business as 'aeronautical engineers and consultants, etc'. There were just two directors on the Board, Elsa Bennett and Mr Howard J Thomson, a solicitor, as AVM Bennett was at this time involved abroad in the formation of British South American Airways Corporation (he was not appointed until 13 September when Mr Thomson duly resigned as director of Fairflight the same day).

Soon after becoming operational one of Fairflight's Tudors was chartered by the Pakistan Government between 28 August and 2 September, while other company aircraft were soon active on charters from their Blackbushe base to the Continent, South Africa and Egypt (where one of the Tudors was reputedly hit by anti-aircraft fire!), and were also engaged for a short time in ferrying Jewish immigrants from Aden to Palestine.

In 1950, however, their activities were set back when, on Sunday 12 March their Tudor 5, G-AKBY, crashed 13 miles west of Cardiff at Sigingstone, Glamorgan whilst on approach to Llandow. In Belfast the day before Wales had won the Triple Crown and the fans were coming home but 75 Welsh rugby supporters and 5 crew died in the crash, in which there were just 3 survivors. The crash received much adverse publicity due to a reported legality regarding the aircraft's C of A and resulted in the company being fined heavily (in 1990 a memorial plaque was erected on the site). Nevertheless, in 1951 the company flew 105,000 revenue miles on freight work carrying a total of 3010 tons, with some 120,000 revenue miles on general work transporting 300 passengers, and in five months on the little Berlin Airlift made 350 return flights to the capital.

Surrey Flying Services Ltd

In October 1951 Freddie Laker, with the intention of furthering his organisations activities, acquired and re-registered Surrey Flying Services Ltd as an operating company with a nominal capital of £5,000, the sole directors being himself and his wife, Joan Mavis Laker. Surrey Flying Services Ltd was one of the oldest established independent airlines, formed in 1921 and operated from Croydon until the end of the Second World War its re-registration was operated in conjunction with Fairflight Ltd. As holdings for the latter had now been sold by AVM Bennett in November 1951 to Surrey Flying Services Ltd Laker and his wife thus became the sole directors of Fairflight Ltd (which was re-registered at 26 Martin Lane on 14 November) on 22 November, with the 99 shares held by AVM Bennett and his wifes' one transferred to Laker and his wife respectively.

At the end of 1951 Surrey Flying Services was operating six heavies using their engineering associates overhaul facilities at Blackbushe and its subsidiary bases at Stansted and Southend, and had flown 20,565 revenue freight miles carrying 509 tons in addition to making 61 return flights between Berlin and Hamburg on the little Berlin Airlift.

Results of this ownership change were realised in July 1952 when, with the total personnel employed by SFS and its associate companies numbering around 300, it was reported that both Fairflight and SFS had in effect amalgamated (although both companies still existed in name) and in future their equipment including Yorks, a Tudor and a Lincoln were to be formed into an Aviation Traders operating company under the name of Air Charter Ltd.

Air Charter Ltd

Contrary to what is generally believed, Air Charter Ltd had originally been registered as a company on 28 May 1946, with a nominal capital of £10,000 in 10,000 £1 shares. There were just two subscribers and two directors, Mr I S T Campbell and Mr G A Phelps, the company being registered at The Aerodrome, Elstree, Hertfordshire, and described as 'being able to conduct and carry out in Great Britain and in other parts of the world, the business of carriers, or pilots of passengers, mails and goods by air; charters of aircraft, managers and operators of airports and aerodromes, etc'.

Their office was re-registered to 120 George Street, Croydon on 7 June 1946, but in July 1947 the company underwent a change of ownership when the two original directors stood down to make way for four new directors, Mr P O Davis, Mr J C Williams, Mr G S Arthur and Mr J Mathieu. These however were all to resign by 14 December 1951, when the company's complete share capital was transferred to Mr Harold Rolf Bamberg of Eagle Aviation and his wife Annis in the ratio of 7,500 and 2,500. The final transfer of company ownership took place six months later on 7 June 1952 when the share capital, in the same ratios, was transferred to Freddie Laker and his wife who were then officially registered as the company directors on 29 August. The registered office was first given as 69 Wigmore Street on 23 July, and subsequently at 40 Mortimer Street, London on 14 October.

Still operational on the Berlin Airlift during December the new company's Yorks recorded 23 passenger trips with 1,150 refugees to Hanover and 47 flights with 370 tons of freight to Hamburg. Air Charter and its associated companies had, in the twelve months up to February 1953, carried one of the biggest cargo totals of any independent operation with a figure of 27,956,000 lbs, believed only to have been surpassed by Silver City. They also carried 9,936 passengers, flew 4,252,768 revenue ton miles and 750,000 revenue miles.

Later, on 21 February 1953, the company took delivery of their first 48-seater Bristol Freighter Mk 31E, G-AMLP, which complemented the fleet of seven Yorks, three Tudors (two of which were out of C of A) and one Dakota. A fourth Tudor, registered in Canada, was leased to Lome Airways whilst still belonging to Air Charter and returned to England on 20 February for overhaul. The company's only unrestricted Tudor 4B, G-AHNM, was fitted with 78 seats (increased from 74) and used solely in Germany. This aircraft was, in terms of economy, described as one of the most economic designs operated into Berlin, its carrying capacity being 9½ metric tons at an all-up weight of 5,000 lbs. Although below its certified maximum, this was more than 2¼ times the capacity of the Dakota.

At this time the company also purchased 17 surplus RAF Yorks which were stripped and re-assembled into as many airworthy aircraft as possible. With these Air Charter then extended its activities in trooping, and in April 1953 were awarded a contract entailing a fortnightly flight to Fiji, followed in May by a contract to fly 2,250 troops weekly into West Africa. In April 1954 they were then awarded a 50% share in a Government trooping contract to carry 16,000 passengers annually to the Canal Zone, flying once-daily in each direction for the 12-month period starting August 1954. One of the Tudors was also used in April to airlift medical supplies into Indo-China.

Hopes that their Tudors would be used for trooping did not materialise as the War Office did not show itself at all willing to accept the types use despite its full C of A and compliance with the 1951 BCA requirements. An exception was for a short period in 1953 when a Fairflight Tudor operated 13 trooping flights to the Canal Zone and Nairobi for the War Office and Air Ministry, during which some 760 passengers were carried and 80,375 statute miles flown without any snags or delays. A Mk 4 was also flown on some simulated trooping runs carrying 13,000 lbs of freight from the UK to Nairobi with only one refuelling stop.

It is possible that reluctance on the part of the War Office to use the Tudor stemmed from the separate disappearances of two BSAAC Tudors while flying near Bermuda, although a clue to these incidents may have been found on 2 March 1954 when, G-AGRI, a Mk 1 of Air Charter, lost control in cloud near Paris on a freight flight from London to Bahrain. After dropping from 9,500 ft Captain J M Carreras finally regained control at 2,500 ft but on reaching Malta the aircraft was found to have been severely overstressed and was taken out of service for a fuller investigation.

The close of 1953 had seen Air Charter's aircraft flying 1,361,524 revenue ton miles with 27,991 tons of freight and 16,494 passengers, and Freddie Laker then decided that the company should try its hand at the vehicle ferrying business. Although the company took delivery of their second Mk 31 Freighter, G-AMSA, on 3 February 1954 it became clear by that summer that, with the ending of the little Berlin Airlift, the company would be hard pressed to find suitable work for the Freighters in just the passenger/freight role.

The Channel Air Bridge

Back in 1952 the aviation industry had always considered Silver City's ideas for a vehicle ferry from Southend to the Continent to be a non-viable proposition, but Freddie Laker however thought differently. It was decided that, in order to give prospective travellers the best and most convenient service to the Continent from Southend, permission would be sort to route via Calais. After preliminary approaches to the ATAC for authority to work this route up to and including 31 August 1964, approval was gained to operate a vehicle ferry service for the carriage of passengers and supplementary freight between 1 September 1954 and 30 June 1961, initially at a frequency of one daily flight in each direction but to be increased according to demand.

The new service, to be known as the 'Channel Air Bridge', was accordingly inaugurated on Wednesday 1 September and to mark the opening a civic party from Southend headed by the Mayor, Councillor H N Bride JP, was invited by Laker to fly to Calais for lunch. On this flight, for which the company's newest Mk 31 Freighter G-ANMF, 'Victory' (delivered on 13 August) was used, the aircraft carried the Mayor's Rolls-Royce (registration number HJ1) and Laker's car, as well as a number of other civic dignitaries including Councillors F H Wood, B Collins, D Fincham, A Nicholl, the Mayor's chauffeur, Mr G Woolmer and two press representatives. On arrival they were met by the town Mayor, M Andre Parmeritier, and the President of Calais Chamber of Commerce, M M Permeuten, toured the sea front and harbour, and were then received at the Town Hall. Mid-September then saw the first official party from the Continent use the Air Bridge when the Southend Mayor responded by welcoming the Calais Mayor and a party of dignitaries, who were invited to attend the traditional Southend Whitebait Festival.

With regard to the actual ferry service, for which the flight time over the 73-mile journey was 28 minutes, the operational frequency was initially four flights daily in each direction which left Southend at 0800, 1030, 1300 and 1530 hrs, with return flights from Calais at 0915, 1145, 1415 and 1645 hrs. The single fare rates were:- for cars up to 12'-6" £7-5s, 12'-6" to 13'-6" £10, 13'-6" to 14'-6" £13, 14'-6" to 15'-6" £15-10s, and over 15'-6" £18. Motorcycles up to 250cc were £2-5s, and over £3, combinations £3-15s, auto cycles and scooters £1-5s, bicycles 7s-6d, power-assisted bicycles and tandems 10s, and tandems with a sidecar 17s-6d. Baggage trailers up to 6'-0" overall length (including the towbar) were charged £3-5s, and those over that were charged 15s per foot. Caravan trailers were priced the same as the overall length rate for cars, and supplementary freight was carried at four pence per kilo. Passenger fares were £2-16s single and £5-1s return, and for those under twelve there was a 50% reduction with those under two years of age travelling free.

During the time the Air Bridge was operational in this first experimental period, in between ferrying cars Air Charter's two Freighters were also engaged in carrying cargoes ranging from pepper and margarine to aircraft parts and new cars for export. Examples of the type of freight carried were 50 drums of margarine brought into Southend from Amsterdam between 25 to 28 October, and 24 cars flown to Dussledorf in the last week of October.

When the ferry was started in September Air Charter had known that there would be the likelihood of Calais Airport being closed for reconstruction between 15 October 1954 and 30 April 1955, however, when they applied to the ATAC for permission to operate to Le Touquet the commission refused to give traffic rights. Nevertheless, during the two months preceding Sunday 31 October, when the last outward flight left Calais before it closed, the operation had proved that there indeed existed a definite market for the service. Plans were therefore made for the coming Spring, when it was their intention to commence the service on 4 April at an increased frequency of 28 flights per day in each direction. What spurred them on was the fact that, during their successful trial period, some 150 cars were carried instead of the expected 50 bookings. Indeed such was Air Charter's jubilation at the results of the services that they felt justified in keeping their Southend enquiry and booking office open over the winter months. This then prompted Southend-on-Sea Town Council, who anticipated a great demand for the coming 1955 services, to approve the expenditure of some £30,000 on redevelopment of the airport facilities.

The end of 1954 had seen Air Charter fly 1,995,055 revenue ton miles, and carry a total of 13,846 passengers and 24,244 tons of freight, and in December the company applied for a ten year licence to operate a vehicle ferry service from Southend to Rotterdam and/or Ypenburg at a frequency of at least one daily flight, dependant on demand. Although no steps were taken in this direction until 1956 (see later), by March 1955 the company were well advanced for the 4 April re-introduction of their Calais service.

On this service, for which the 1954 tariffs were still applied, the company also introduced an incentive scheme by which fares totalling £20 or more could be paid for over a period of six to nine months. The service frequency during the season was also increased until, between 4 and 30 April, there were seven return services daily plus six additional daily return trips during the Easter week of 6 to 13 April. This schedule was then increased to 16 round trips from 1 to 20 May, 24 between 21 and 31 May, 32 between 1 June and 18 September, and thereafter 24 round trips daily until the end of September.

To assist in running the service Air Charter took delivery on 25 March and 5 April of two long-nosed Mk 32 Freighters, G-ANVR and 'NVS, which then supplemented the existing fleet of three Mk 31 Freighters, seven Yorks (four by November 1955), eleven Tudors and one Douglas C54. The sole C54, G-ANYB (later to become the Carvair prototype) had been delivered to Stansted from New York via Shannon on 25 January 1955 and was the first of three brought in to expand the company's trooping activities. The other two British C54s registered in December 1955 were G-AOXK and 'OFW, the latter having been delivered to Hanover from Rome on 11 December for overhaul before being used in Berlin (and later became Carvair no 11).

With the reintroduction of CAB's Calais service in April 1955 the extension work being carried out by Southend Corporation to enable the airport to cope with the anticipated increase in vehicle ferry traffic was well advanced. The work included constructing concrete hardstands and finishing off the new runway works (this having commenced on Tuesday, 20 September 1954), as well as erecting a shed for car and Customs handling, and doubling the size of the 1951-built passenger handling buildings to include a new reception hall, information desks and a restaurant. Air Charter also added to these extensions by erecting their own car petrol filling station.

Around this time Air Charter had applied for permission to operate a new ferry service between Southend and Ostende, initially with a daily winter frequency of one flight in each direction. The service was duly approved for operation up to and including 30 June 1961 and opened to the public on Tuesday, 18 October 1955, but had been officially inaugurated the day before using the company's Mk 31E, G-AMLP. On this flight were Freddie Laker and Mrs Laker, the Southend Mayor, Alderman Mrs C Leyland OBE, JP, Councillor F H Woods, chairman of the airport committee and other Corporation officials, along with two cars, one of which was the Mayor's Rolls Royce.

"Something from the trolley, sir?" The variety of tax-free goods was limited to spirits and cigarettes, here seen being offered for selection in this posed shot for CAB in the late-50s. The aircraft is Freighter G-AMLP 'Vanguard', with passengers in the new style of seating fitted on conversion from the Mk 31E to 32 (photo by Geroy, Southend).

The 250,000th car loading into SCA Freighter Mk 32 G-AMWH 'City of Hereford' at Lydd in June 1959 for Le Touquet with the Kents and Milners of Sutton Coldfield as passengers (SCA photo).

New Rootes Group left-hand drive cars being loaded into CAB Freighter Mk 32 G-ANVS 'Vigilant' at Southend for export. This was one of the many lucrative contracts carried out by the air ferry companies (photo by Geroy).

One of the many notable persons to use the car ferry, actor George Sanders, his wife (the former Mrs Ronald Coleman) and her daughter Juliet, watch their car being loaded into a Freighter Mk 32 of CAB at Southend in July 1959 for their return home to Switzerland after a three-week English holiday (photo by Highlands Studios).

Publicity shot of left-hand drive Daimler sports cars awaiting loading into CAB Freighter Mk 32 G-AMLP 'Vanguard' at Southend for export on 22 March 1961 (ATEL photo).

Even after the Carvair entered service the 'Biffo' was still in use. Here the Rootes Group Sunbeam Alpine entries for the Le Mans 24-hour race are being loaded into Freighter Mk 32 G-ANWK 'City of Leicester' of British United Air Ferries at Hurn for Cherbourg on 9 June 1963 (Rootes Motors Ltd photo).

Seen from SCA Freighter Mk 32 G-AMWD 'City of Leicester', 'MWA 'City of London' taxies out for departure, hiding 'MWB 'City of Salisbury', on a rain-soaked apron at Le Touquet in August 1960 (photo by Ken Honey).

Bristol Freighter G-AMLP after conversion to Mk 32 standard, in the colours of British United and carrying the name 'Super Bristol' on the tail at Southend in 1966 (from the Paul Purser collection).

On landing at Middlekerke Airport after the 40-minute flight the guests were met by the Burgermaster of Ostende, Monsieur Titeca and taken by car to the Palais de Justice – the town's temporary Town Hall while their new one was being built. On arrival greetings were exchanged between Alderman Leyland and the Burgermaster, the latter then presented the former with a plaque to commemorate the occasion. Following the reception the party was then lunched by Air Charter and entertained to tea at the home of the British Vice-Consul before being flown back to Southend together with the routes' first farepaying passenger.

The service frequency was then increased to ten flights daily in each direction in the spring of 1956, the aircraft being initially scheduled to depart from Southend at 1300 and Ostende at 1510 hrs with a flying time of 39 minutes. The single fare rates had gained approval by the IATA on 13 October and were:- cars up to 12'-6" £12-10s, 12'-6" to 13'-6" £15-15s, 13'-6" to 14'-6" £18, 14'-6" to 15'-6" £20-15s, and over 15'-6" £23-10s; motorcycles up to 250cc £3, over 250cc £4-10s, combinations and tricars £5-15s, autocycles and scooters £1-17s-6d, power assisted cycles and tandems £1, tandem with sidecar £1-15s, bicycles 15s, baggage trailers up to 6'-0" £4-4s, over 6'-0" 15s per foot (including towbar). Fares for passengers were £4-4s single, with a 50% reduction for children under 12, and children under 2 years old travelled at 10% of the respective adult fare.

Following the establishment of their Ostende service, the start of which coincided neatly with Southend's new terminal complex being officially opened by the Minister of Transport, Mr J Boyd Carpenter, Air Charter then announced their intention to operate a Southend to Rotterdam vehicle ferry service as from 1 October 1956. This tied in with their application to carry 'without restriction any passengers not associated with cars' on the Calais route, and complimented the approval already gained for the Ostende service.

During 1955, a year that saw one of Air Charter's Yorks crashing when its undercarriage collapsed on landing at Southend on 21 September, the fleet was generally kept very busy. The five Freighters were used exclusively on the vehicle ferry services and general cargo charters, while additionally two C54s, four Yorks and five Super Traders were operated. Three of the Traders were being converted and also on order were two more Bristol Freighters and a C54.

However, whilst there was much interest in the new C54s, and the boost these would give to the long haul trooping and passenger charters, one of the most notable flights during this period was on 1 September when one of the Freighters carried to Ostende what was at that time the largest-recorded, commercially-airlifted lorry to be flown from this country. The six-ton monster, from Rotary Hoes Ltd of East Horndon, was loaded with Howard 'Rotavators' for a demonstration tour of Belgium.

As to Air Charter's vehicle ferry services, during the peak holiday period of 1955 up to 32 daily flights were operated on the Calais route, this being highlighted between Thursday 26 and Saturday 28 May when a total of 200 cars was flown to and from the French port. In total the company carried 13,846 passengers, and flew 33,264 tons of freight amounting to 3,365,929 revenue ton miles, while on the Calais vehicle ferry service between 1 September 1954 and 30 September 1955, they operated 3,712 services carrying 19,286 passengers, 6,965 vehicles and 38 tons of freight, their aircraft flying 747,701 revenue ton miles. Also in the 1955 calendar year the company flew 532 and 15 revenue ton miles respectively on the Calais and Ostende vehicle ferry services.

By January 1956, when Southend's new concrete runway was nearing completion with over 1,400 yards laid, the justification of such expense became apparent the following February. Due to excessive rain during the early part of the month, coupled with some generally mild weather not associated with that time of year, Southend's existing grass runways became completely waterlogged and unserviceable and Air Charter were obliged to operate services out of Stansted. With this revision to their services the company then received approval during June for an amendment to the terms of their vehicle ferry service operating between Southend and Rotterdam and/or Ypenburg. This change allowed them to operate up to two return flights daily up to 7 July 1962, with approval to carry up to 12 passengers not associated with vehicles, instead of six as originally authorised.

When the hard runway came into use at Southend another in-service snag with the Bristol Freighter was eliminated, this being the possibility of the clamshell nose doors unlatching when the aircraft was operating over uneven grass surfaces. Instances of this had occurred to Captains Ian Peyton and 'Lofty' Coupton taking off in G-ANVS (both doors unlatched and, on opening back with the airflow, smashed into both propellors and brought about an abrupt end to the flight), and a French crew who suffered a similar problem at Calais.

On 1 July the company started a new integrated freighting service known as 'Trukair' in conjunction with Atlas Air Services. This express carrier service, which had already been co-ordinated throughout the UK by Atlas, was now combined with Air Charter's vehicle ferry services to form a service similar to Silver City's 'Roadair' operation started in 1955. By this goods could be collected and delivered door-to-door in the UK and the Continent with reciprocal road transport used to ensure a maximum transit time between destinations not exceeding 40 hours.

Air Charter's Rotterdam vehicle ferry service, the buildup for which is described earlier, was duly inaugurated on 1 October some two weeks after the first car had actually been flown by the company's Mk 31 Freighter, G-AMSA, when at Rotterdam on 18 September a three-day old Ford Consul was loaded into the aircraft from the back of a lorry as the specialised loading ramps had not yet arrived from England.

On 1 October, coincident with the official opening of Rotterdam's new airport facilities, Mr J Klaasesz, Queen Juliana's Commissioner for the Province of South Holland, gave a speech which was televised and reported by journalists from all over Europe. Part of the ceremony included a special message from London's Lord Mayor to the Burgermaster of Rotterdam which a Mr A Mihado, a Dutch radio commentor from London, had brought across on the Air Bridge. This had been done in order to win a wager that it was possible, by making use of the service, to drive from the Mansion House, London to the centre of Amsterdam in under three hours. Things however did not turn out that easy for although Mihado was guided en route by an official lady pilot from the AA, with his progress broadcast over Dutch radio by commentators based at Southend, their car ultimately arrived late there due to traffic delays. However, and to keep up the spirit of the adventure, Freddie Laker sent the crew of Freighter G-ANVS 'Vigilant' to fly with all possible speed to Rotterdam, such that the message was delivered with just two minutes to spare, the aircraft touching down in Holland at 1217 hrs after a 64-minute flight.

The inaugural flight of the Rotterdam service on 1 October carried a number of Southend dignitaries including Councillor F H Woods, chairman of the airport committee, Councillor R Smith, chairman of the publicity committee and Councillor F G Feather, chairman of the finance committee, along with press representatives. It was also loaded with two cars, one being the Mayor's Rolls Royce, which caused great interest on arrival just as it had done previously when carried on both the Calais and Ostende inaugural flights.

The party were met on arrival by the Burgermaster Mr G E Van Walsum LLD, and driven through Rotterdam to a reception with an escort of motorcycle police. That same day East Anglian Flying Services, another local company, were inaugurating their Southend/Ipswich to Rotterdam passenger service and had earlier that morning flown Southend's Mayor, H H Smith JP, over in a company Dove.

At the reception Mr J A C Tillema, the contractor in charge of building the new terminal at Rotterdam, told the guests, including the Mayor of Ipswich and General Aler, President of KLM, that work started on the airport on 18 May 1954, and in August 1955 Rotterdam was given Government sanction to construct a new 4,250 ft by 150 ft wide runway. The inaugural programme included a boat trip around the harbour with lunch taken on board, followed by a tour of the city and an evening banquet attended by nearly 1,000 people.

Previous to this the places of British journalists on the aircraft's arrival at Rotterdam had been taken by Dutch colleagues including a TV newsreel team. They were duly flown to Southend and, following a telephone call from Rotterdam by the Southend Town Clerk, were met by the town's publicity officer, Mr L A W Jones. Afterwards several films taken of Southend were later shown on Dutch TV. Air Charter also returned to Southend with 2,000 choice blooms which had been presented to Southend by the Co-operative Auction of Cut Flowers of the 'Westland Region' of Holland. Later, on Wednesday 3 October, Dutch hospitality was repaid when the Burgermeister of Rotterdam and the town council members were flown via the Air Bridge to Southend, to be met on arrival by the Mayor.

The scheduled service, for which the flight time over the 165-mile route was 69 minutes, was initially opened by Air Charter with two flights in each direction for the winter season (1 October to 31 March 1957), which left Southend at 0915 and 1600, and Rotterdam at 1200 and 1845 hrs. As to carriage rates, single fares for cars varied between £14 and £30, motorcycles over 250cc were £4-10s, under 250cc £3-15s, combinations and tri-cars £7, autocycles and scooters £2, and bicycles 3s-6d. Passengers were charged £6-5s single and £11-5s return.

Following this, Air Charter was now operating all three vehicle ferry services, and in total between 1 October 1955 and 30 September 1956 they completed 5,988 services carrying 31,827 passengers, 10,261 vehicles and 613 tons of freight, their aircraft having flown 986,951 revenue ton miles. In the 1956 calendar year the company also flew 608, 209 and 33 revenue ton miles respectively on the Calais, Ostende and Rotterdam services.

Of the charters carried out by the vehicle ferry division during 1956 the most prestigious was on 25 April when a black and grey coloured Rolls Royce, due to be presented by the Conceil Nationale de Monaco to his Serene Highness Prince Rainier on the occasion of his wedding to the former starlet Miss Grace Kelly, duly adorned with the Prince's crown and cypher on its door panels, was flown across to France from Southend. Another interesting charter during the summer saw the companies' Mk 31, G-AMSA, fly a dismantled Sikorsky S-51 helicopter, G-AJOR of Autair, to Mestervig, Greenland, an exercise repeated by Silver City the following year.

As an incentive for the 1956 season Air Charter reduced rates for cars between 12'-6" and 12'-9" in length, to cater for such types as the Ford Popular, Anglia and Prefect series, most Triumph TR's and the Singer Roadster. The fare structure on their Calais service was also revised and regrouped into two categories - Standard and Off-Peak. The Standard period applied between 13 July and 9 September, the fares being - cars between £7-15s and £18-5s, motorcycles up to 250cc were £2-15s (£2-10s), over 250cc £3-5s (£3-0s), three-wheelers and sidecars £4-15s (£4-5s), scooters and mopeds £1-10s (£1-7s-6d), and motorised cycles 3s-6d (bracketed figures applied to the Off-Peak period). Passenger fares were £3-5s single and £5-18s return, with children at £1-12s-6d single and £2-19s return.

With only minor adjustments these fare scales worked and Air Charter's activities continued under the flag of the Channel Air Bridge, still using the Freighter for the vehicle ferry whilst their other types were employed on pure freight and passenger work, and by the end of 1962 some 138,000 cars and 565,000 passengers had been carried. 1 January 1963 saw the demise of Silver City Airways and the two companies merged to form British United, subsequently it became British United Air Ferries, with the main operating bases now limited to Southend, Lydd and Southampton. Proposed routes from Lydd and Southend to Coventry, Liege and Paris did not materialise, and as the air ferries lost more cross-Channel business to the shipping ferries so route withdrawals became more frequent. A further name change brought in British Air Ferries, which carried on the vehicle ferry operations from Southend only until the mid-1970s, by which time service demand had dwindled. After a period of passenger and pure freight work using the Carvair aircraft then in use these were put up for disposal.

The air ferry story using the Carvair as the operating aircraft is given in the companion volume 'Air Bridge 2', to which the reader may wish to refer.

Conclusions

The story of the vehicle air ferry is, without doubt, the story of Silver City Airways, and its struggles to expand its activities in what was at the time a new use for air transport. Whilst Silver City had, as a group, increased in size by absorbing most of the smaller and useful operators it did not enjoy as much success in furthering its aircraft suitability.

Nevertheless, without Silver City, and all its contemporaries who used the Bristol Freighter as the only air ferry vehicle available to them at the time, as well as its successors, but particularly British United Air Ferries who brought in the innovative and necessary ATL98 *'Carvair'* conversions of the Douglas C54 design, there would have been no continuation of the cross-Channel vehicle air ferry, that enabled the concept to last eventually for close on twenty-five years.

The success of the car ferry was mainly due to the distance to the French airfields 'on the other side', say 37 nautical miles from Lydd to Le Touquet, such that if an aircraft (or even two) went out of service on the 'bridge' it was possible to catch up on services, as well as being able to get a relief out as well. If a serious breakdown occurred, through weather or otherwise, it was not too far to divert to the boat ferries at Dover or Folkestone.

The struggles experienced by Silver City can be likened to the well-known press picture of Freddie Laker holding a model Concorde with the caption "give me this plane and I'll make it pay". Silver City tried long and hard to find a successor to the Freighter, but the many types designed or trialled were not taken up for various reasons. For survival of the vehicle air ferry any new idea had to be tried and as Concorde was 're-born', after the disasterous crash at Paris in 1999, so the air ferry had its own re-birth with the arrival of the Carvair.

I only experienced the last ten years of the 'air bridge' but I must say to all the men and women who worked on the 'bridge', and the aircraft used, you all worked well and have truly written many pages in the history of air transport. There will never be another era like it.

In closing I must pay tribute to some of the cross-Channel airbridge crews, and apologise for not having all of their full names, some of these details having been provided from memory by Anthony English (thanks for the salmon sandwiches and champagne). They are:-

Richard Besley, Jim Broadbent, Peter Cheal, 'Lofty' Coupton, Messrs Cullum, Cussons and Damon, M Davison, Tony English, Dave Flett, C Helliwell, George Hogarth, Ken Honey, C I Hopkins, Cyril Hopwood, David Hutchinson, Messrs Jones and Knight, Len Lakey, Bob Langley, Len Madelaine, Messrs Lawson, Mattock, Salmon, Thompson and Zweibergk, Jack Norton, Ian Peyton, Eddie Ruecroft, Gerry Rosser, Peter Treadaway and Joe Viatkin.

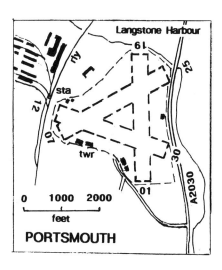

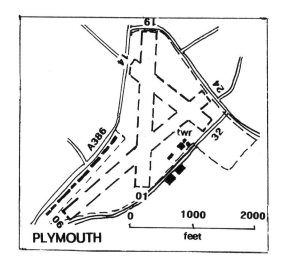

Comparison in low-level cross-Channel routing
(Extracted from Pooleys Air Touring Flight Guides for United Kingdom & Europe)

1962

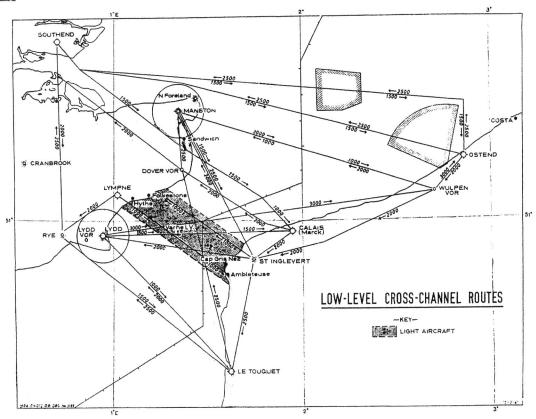

1971

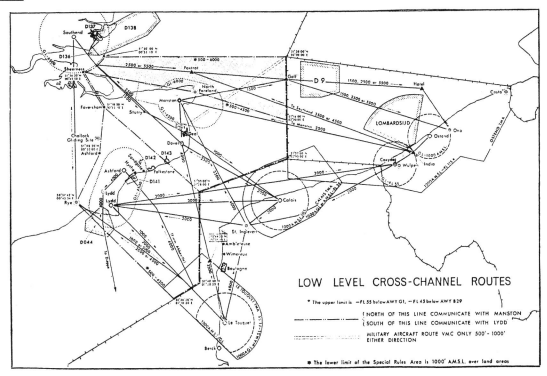

Appendix 1   Conversion tables

Currency

(examples)	¾d	6d	1s	2s	5s	8s	10s	13s	14s	14s-6d	15s	18s	19s
		0.3p	2½p	5p	10p	25p	40p	50p	65p	70p	72½p	75p	90p	95p

Length

(examples)	6"		1'-0"	6'-10"	8'-0"	10'-0"	12'-0"	13'-6"	15'-0"
		0.152m	0.304m	2.08m	2.44m	3.05m	3.66m	4.12m	4.57m

Weights

(examples)   1 kg = 2.204 lbs, 1 ton = 2240 lbs (1016 kgs), 1 'short' ton = 2000 lbs

Appendix 2   Data for Bristol Freighter aircraft

	Mk 1 Freighter	Mk 32 'Superfreighter'
Span	98ft 0in	108ft 0in
Length	68ft 4in	73ft 8in
Height	21ft 8in	24ft 0in
Wing area	1,405ft²	1,487ft²
Empty weight	23,482lbs	29,465lbs
All-up weight	36,500lbs	44,000lbs
Maximum speed	240 kts	195 kts
Cruising speed	163 kts	165 kts
Initial climb	1,420ft/min	1,000ft/min
Ceiling	22,000ft	24,500ft
Range (max load)	300 nm	700 nm
Range (max fuel)	462 nm	1610 nm.

Variants		
	Mk 1	Freighter, freight-carrying version with nose doors, Bristol Hercules 632 engines
	Mk 1A	Freighter, as Mk 1 but with cargo hold forward and 16 passenger seats to the rear
	Mk 2	Freighter, no nose doors, large freight loading door each side of fuselage
	Mk 2A	Wayfarer, no nose doors, 36 (max) passenger seats
	Mk 2C	Wayfarer, combined 20 passenger/freight fore and aft
	Mk 11A	prototype of new type 170, wingspan increased by 10ft
	Mk 21	Freighter, as Mk 2A but higher weights, Bristol Hercules 672 engines
	Mk 21A	Freighter, forward freight hold and 16 seats in rear
	Mk 21E	Freighter, mixed passenger/freight role with moveable bulkhead
	Mk 21M	Freighter, military version of Mk 21
	Mk 22A	Wayfarer, 36 passenger seats, Hercules 672 engines
	Mk 31	Freighter, modified tail unit, dorsal fin, other mods, Hercules 734 engines
	Mk 31E	Freighter, mixed passenger/freight role with moveable bulkhead, Hercules 734 engines
	Mk 31M	Freighter, military version of Mk 31, Hercules 734 engines
	Mk 32	Superfreighter, lengthened nose, 3 cars, 20 passengers, Hercules 734 engines.

Appendix 3   General arrangements of Bristol 170 Freighter aircraft

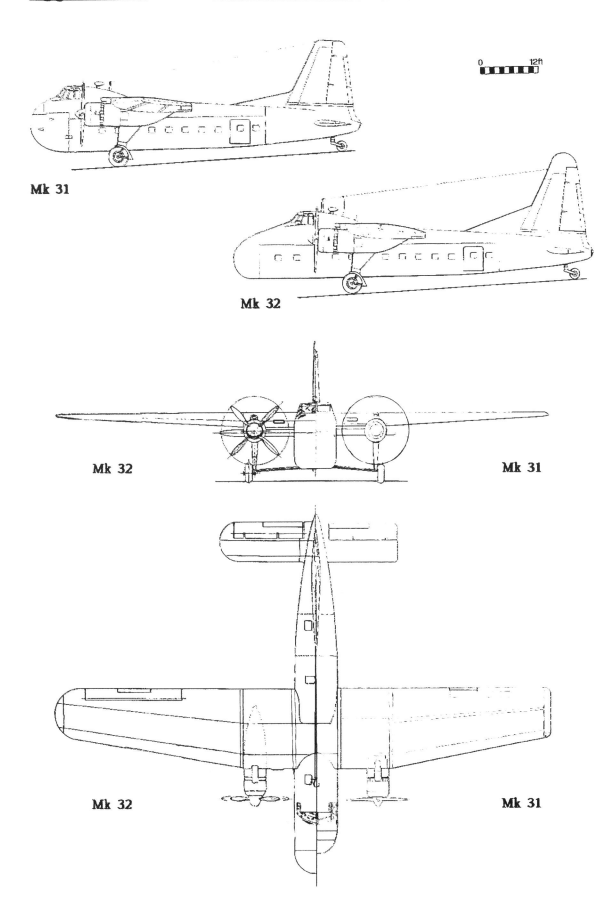

Mk 31

Mk 32

Mk 32   Mk 31

Mk 32   Mk 31

0   12ft

Appendix 4   Silver City Airways vehicle ferry services from 1948 to 1954

Year	Service	Remarks
1948	Lympne → Le Touquet	Charter basis only between 13 July to 7 October.
1949	-do-	Scheduled service from 13 April to 29 October, then on-demand until 1 April 1950.
1950	-do-	Scheduled service from 1 April.
1951	-do-	Yearly scheduled service.
1951/2	Southampton (Eastleigh) → Cherbourg (Maupertus)	Demonstration flight on 5 December, seasonal scheduled service inaugurated 1 February 1952.
1952	Lympne → le Touquet	As for 1951.
	Southend → Brussels	Demonstration flight only 30 January.
	Southend → Ostende (Middlekerke)	Demonstration flight 31 January, service started 14 April but discontinued end-April.
	Southampton → Guernsey and/or Jersey	Application only March, re-submitted in July 1954.
	Lympne → Ostende	Seasonal on-demand service started end-April to replace the Southend to Ostende service (above).
	Southampton → Isle of Wight	Report only in April.
	Blackpool (Squires Gate) → Isle of Man	Proposal to operate a limited service, in conjunction with Lancashire Aircraft Corporation, but did not materialise.
	UK → Paris	Proposed deep-penetration service.
1953	Lympne → Le Touquet	As for 1952.
	Lympne → Ostende	As for 1952.
	Southampton → Cherbourg	As for 1952.
	Tripoli (Idris-el-Awal) → Benghazi (Benina)	Scheduled service (flagged as Libyan Airways) inaugurated 1 February, discontinued in June 1954.
	Belfast → Stranraer	Report only in February.
	Birmingdon (Elmdon) → Le Touquet	Demonstration flight 6 May, scheduled service started 17 June 1955 but discontinued August 1955.
	London (Gatwick) → Le Touquet	Proving flight 15 April, seasonal scheduled service started 15 May.
	Southampton → Isle of Wight	Proving flight 2 July, on-demand service started 3 July but discontinued in August.
1954	Southampton → Isle of Wight (Ryde)	Application only in January.
	London (Blackbushe) → Zurich (Kloten)	Three-month experimental seasonal winter service started 2 January but discontinued later.
	Lympne → Le Touquet	As for 1953 up to 13 July when discontinued.
	Lympne → Ostende	As for 1953 up to 3 October when discontinued.
	Southampton → Cherbourg	As for 1953.
	Lympne → Calais (Marck)	Seasonal scheduled service from 1 June until 3 October.
	London → Le Touquet	As for 1953.
	Lydd (Ferryfield) → Le Touquet	Service started 14 July to replace the Lympne to Le Touquet service (above).
	Lympne or Lydd → Calais /Ostende/Le Touquet and Boulogne	Approval gained in August to operate a helicopter vehicle and freight ferry but the service did not materialise.
	Lydd → Basle	Application only made in October.
	Lydd and/or Southampton → Le Havre or Deauville	Application only in October, Le Havre route not taken up
	Stranraer (West Freugh) → Belfast (Newtownards)	Application only made in December.
	London (Blackbushe) → Belfast via Birmingham and Woodvale (Liverpool)	Application only made in December.

Appendix 5

Silver City Airways Timetable for 1953 summer season
(example - as published in the ABC World Airways Guide)

LONDON (Gatwick) → LE TOUQUET

miles	X		X		X		X
0	1230	/	1830	dep LONDON arr ↑	1135	/	1735
91	1305	/	1905	↓ arr LE TOUQUET dep	1100	/	1700

FOLKESTONE (Lympne) → OSTEND (Middlekerke)

miles	X	every	X		X	every	X
0	0800	2 hrs	1600	dep FOLKESTONE arr ↑	0935	2 hrs	1735
99	0835	until	1635	↓ arr OSTEND del	0900	until	1700

SOUTHAMPTON (Eastleigh) - BEMBRIDGE (Isle of Wight)

miles	X	every	X		X	every	X
0	1015	60 mins	1815	dep SOUTHAMPTON arr ↑	1054	60 mins	1854
21	1024	until	1824	↓ arr BEMBRIDGE del	1045	until	1845

SOUTHAMPTON (Eastleigh) - CHERBOURG (Maupertus)

miles	X	every	X		X	every	X
0	0800	75 mins	1645	dep SOUTHAMPTON arr ↑	0950	75 mins	1835
88	0835	until	1720	↓ arr CHERBOURG del	0915	until	1800

FOLKESTONE (Lympne) - LE TOUQUET

miles	X	every	X		X	every	X
0	0715	15 mins	2015	dep FOLKESTONE arr ↑	0820	15 mins	2120
47	0735	until	2035	↓ arr LE TOUQUET del	0800	until	2100

During the winter period the Gatwick-Le Touquet and Lympne-Ostend services were suspended, with the Lympne-Le Touquet reduced to a 30-minute, each way operation.

Appendix 6

Silver City Airways statistics from 1948 to 1954

(vehicle ferry services only)	1948	1949	1950	1951
Cars	170	2600	3253	7529
Motorcycles	–	100	639	3240
Bicycles	–	–	127	1355
Vehicle total	170	2700	4019	12124
Passengers	350	7900	10800	30137
Vehicle payload (short tons)	229	3538	4616	11456
Freight other than vehicles	13	250	329	829
Total freight payload	242	3788	4945	12285

	1952	1953	1954
Cars	6896	24063	30966
Motorcycles	2203	8227	7431
Bicycles	1842	6751	4110
Vehicle total	10941	39041	42507
Passengers	28836	96625	112214
Vehicle payload (short tons)	10361	36356	44941
Freight other than vehicles	10219	11538	6594
Total freight payload	20580	47894	51535

Statistics given are those generally accepted as correct for the period from 1 January to 31 December each year. Some publications gave conflicting totals, arising from different time windows being used. After 1954 figures were usually given up to 30 September each year.

Appendix 7   Silver City Airways vehicle ferry services from 1955 to 1962

Year	Service	Remarks
1955	Lydd(Ferryfield) → Le Touquet (Paris Plage)	Yearly scheduled service.
	Lydd → Calais (Marck)	Resumption of 1954 Lympne to Calais seasonal service.
	Lydd → Ostende (Middlekerke)	Resumption of 1954 Lympne to Ostende seasonal service.
	London (Gatwick) → Le Touquet	Seasonal service as in 1954.
	Southampton (Eastleigh) → Cherbourg (Maupertus)	Seasonal service as in 1954.
	Southampton → Deauville	Seasonal service to St Gatien, inaugurated 6/4/55.
	Stranraer (Castle Kennedy) → Belfast (Newtownards)	Yearly service inaugurated 7/4/55 to replace December 1954 application using West Freugh.
	London (Blackbushe) → Belfast	Service proposed to start 5/4/55 but postponed after proving flights in April 1955.
	UK → Eire	Report only in April 1955.
	Birmingham (Elmdon) → Le Touquet	Inaugurated 17/6/55 but discontinued in August 1955.
	Liverpool (Woodvale) → Belfast	On-demand service inaugurated 17/6/55 but discontinued in December 1955.
	Lydd → Calais	'Roadair' freight service introduced 1/11/55.
	Lydd → Basle	Winter sports enthusiasts service, first flight on 16/12/55 carried out then discontinued.
1956	Lydd → Le Touquet	As for 1955.
	Lydd → Calais	Service revised to a yearly scheduled operation.
	Lydd → Ostende	As for 1955.
	London → Le Touquet	As for 1955 until October when discontinued.
	Southampton → Cherbourg	As for 1955.
	Southampton → Deauville	As for 1955.
	Stranraer → Belfast	As for 1955 but with increased frequency.
	Lydd → Calais	Application made March 1956 for 'Roadair' service to be operated in conjunction with vehicle ferry service.
	Southampton → Guernsey (La Villiaze)	Yearly scheduled vehicle ferry and freight service inaugurated 27/2/56.
	Isle of Man (Ronaldsway) → Stranraer and Belfast	Application only April 1956. Freight carried between Isle of Man and Belfast May 1956.
	London (Victoria Coach Station) → Paris (Gare du Nord) via Le Touquet	'Silver Arrow' coach-air-rail seasonal scheduled service, proving flight 17/5/56, inaugurated 18/5/56.
	London → Brussels via Ostende	'Silver Arrow' coach-air-rail seasonal scheduled service, inaugurated 14/5/56.
	Stranraer → Belfast (Sydenham)	Temporary use of Sydenham in place of Newtownards from 17/5/56.
	Southampton → Jersey	Experimental two month service inaugurated 13/7/56, run in conjunction with Guernsey service.
	Belfast → Isle of Man	Report only for service to be operated from 3/8/56, and later from September 1956.
	Lydd → Calais/Le Touquet and Southampton → Deauville/Cherbourg/ Jersey and Guernsey	Expansion of 'Roadair' freight service to include all cross Channel vehicle ferry and freight routes, September 1956.
	Cherbourg → Guernsey and/or Jersey	Freight/vehicle ferry approved October 1956, freight only started October 1956 between Guernsey and Cherbourg.
	London (Battersea) → Paris (Le Bourget)	'Roadair' through-freight service started December 1956.

Appendix 7 (Continued)

Year	Service	Remarks
1957	Lydd → Le Touquet	As for 1956.
	Lydd → Calais	As for 1956.
	Lydd → Ostende	Service revised to a yearly operation.
	Stranraer → Belfast	As for 1956 until discontinued in November.
	Southampton → Jersey and Guernsey	Combined freight and vehicle ferry service until October when both discontinued.
	Southampton → Cherbourg	As for 1956.
	Southampton → Deauville	As for 1956.
	'Roadair' services	As for 1956.
	London → Paris	'Silver Arrow' service, operated as 1956 from 12/4/57.
	London → Brussels	'Silver Arrow' service, resumed from 17/5/57 with the coach service between Ostende and Brussels replaced by a train journey, discontinued October 1957. (the 'Silver Arrow' services were operated in conjunction with Linjebuss European Coach Services)
	Belfast → Isle of Man (Jurby)	Report in March of one-day service on 7/7/57 started on 1/6/57 for a limited period but routed into Ronaldsway.
	Stranraer → Isle of Man	Approval gained July but service did not materialise.
1958	Lydd → Le Touquet	As for 1957.
	Lydd → Calais	As for 1957.
	Lydd → Ostende	As for 1957.
	Southampton → Cherbourg	As for 1957.
	Southampton → Deauville	As for 1957.
	London → Paris	'Silver Arrow' service, revised schedule between London and Lydd, also used Super-Wayfarer on cross-Channel element from 21/5/58.
	'Roadair' services	As for 1957 with a change to the direct Southampton to Guernsey/Jersey operation and an extra service between London (Chelsea Bridge) to Lille/Roubaix and Tourcoing areas of France from July 1958, also an extension from November for a car delivery contract.
1959	Lydd → Le Touquet	As for 1958.
	Lydd → Calais	As for 1958.
	Lydd → Ostende	As for 1958.
	Bournemouth (Hurn) → Cherbourg	Seasonal service in lieu of Southampton to Cherbourg, operated from 11 March to 13 June then resumed from Southampton, discontinued from the latter in October.
	Bournemouth → Deauville	Seasonal service in lieu of Southampton to Deauville, operated from 4 June to 13 June then resumed from Southampton, but discontinued in October.
	Lydd → Le Touquet	Experimental cheap-day 'no-passport' service operated from 31 March to 30 September. Extension to service inaugurated 2 June between London (Victoria Coach Station) and Lydd designated 'wheels and wings' service.
	London → Paris	'Silver Arrow' service, new seasonal schedule via Manston using Hermes a/c on cross-Channel flight, from 15/6/59. Carried into winter period on a single daily flight basis.
	Southampton → Jersey via Cherbourg	New winter extension of previous service inaugurated on 5 October but transferred to Hurn 18 November.
	'Roadair' services	As for 1958, but with Southampton services transferred to Hurn along with the vehicle ferry services.
	Anglesey (Valley or Mona) → Dublin	Application made in March but service did not materialise although 1 September 1960 was the probable start date.
	Lydd and/or Manston → Paris (Cormeilles/Cologne and Auxerre	Application made in May but approval given to operate to only Troyes/Pontoise (for Paris) and Cologne, application amended but services did not materialise.

Year	Service	Remarks
1960	Lydd → Le Touquet	As for 1959.
	Lydd → Calais	As for 1959.
	Lydd → Ostende	As for 1959 until 1/4/60 when transferred to Manston, but resumed from Lydd 1/12/60.
	Hurn → Cherbourg	Continuation of 1959 service from March.
	Lydd → Deauville	Seasonal service inaugurated 1 June for limited period and subsequently discontinued.
	London → Paris via Lydd	'No-passport' service introduced 15 June in conjunction with Inter City Tours.
	London → Paris	'Silver Arrow' service as for 1959 but with increased frequency, discontinued from Manston 1 October.
	Blackpool (Squires Gate) → Isle of Man	Application only in June, service did not materialise.
	'Roadair' services	As for 1959 but with an extra link in October between London (Chelsea Bridge) and Hurn in connection with the existing Hurn to Jersey 'Roadair' service.
	Le Touquet and/or Calais and/or Cherbourg → Leeds/Bradford, Blackpool and/or Liverpool and/or Manchester, Glasgow and/or Edinburgh, Newcastle, and Newcastle → Amsterdam	Applications only in October, services did not materialise.
1961	Lydd → Le Touquet	As for 1960.
	Lydd → Calais	As for 1960.
	Lydd → Ostende	Continued from Lydd as for 1959.
	Hurn → Cherbourg	As for 1960.
	Guernsey → Cherbourg	Scheduled service introduced February but with increased frequency from 9 September.
	London → Paris	'Silver Arrow' service re-operated from Lydd with the HP Hermes a/c from 23 June.
	'Roadair' services	As for 1960.
	Lydd or Manston → Basle	Application rejected as BUA favoured on route.
	Manston/Hurn/London → Marseilles & Genoa	Application rejected as BEA and BUA favoured on route.
	Manston/Hurn/London → Lisbon & Madeira	Application rejected as BUA favoured on route.
1962	Lydd → Le Touquet	As for 1961.
	Lydd → Calais	As for 1961.
	Lydd → Ostende	As for 1961.
	Hurn → Cherbourg	As for 1961.
	Guernsey → Cherbourg	As for 1961.
	London → Paris	'Silver Arrow' service as for 1961.
	'Roadair' services	As for 1961.
	Newcastle → Le Touquet and/or Calais and/or Cherbourg	Licence application revoked.
	Lydd or Manston → Le Touquet & Troyes	Licence application revoked.
	Lydd or Manston → Le Touquet & Pentoise	Licence application revoked.
	Blackpool and/or Manchester and/or Liverpool → Le Touquet and/or Calais and/or Cherbourg	Route licence suspended.

Year	Service	Remarks
1962 contd	Leeds/Bradford → Le Touquet and/or Calais and/or Cherbourg	Route licence suspended.
	Bournemouth or Gatwick or Lydd → Deauville or Le Havre	Route licence suspended.
	Newcastle → Amsterdam	Route licence suspended.

Note: Particular airport names are not repeated if they are the same as previous services or other route licence applications to the same location.

The services do not include those gained when Silver City took over Air Kruise's coach-air and inclusive-tour services, or the SCA passenger division operations not aligned with vehicle ferry services, these details can be found in the main text.

Appendix 8   Silver City Airways statistics from 1955 to 1962

(vehicle ferry services only)	1955(1)	1956	1957	1958(2)
Cars	44670	33191	34361	50006
Motorcycles	8774	n/k	n/k	4826
Bicycles	3657	n/k	n/k	1200
Vehicle total	57101	44848	43002	56032
Passengers	166219	125243	117178	153760

	1959(3)	1960(4)	1961(5)	1962(6)
Cars	67452	90332	87466	96272
Motorcycles	4826	n/k	n/k	n/k
Bicycles	n/k	n/k	n/k	n/k
Vehicle total	67452	90332	87466	96272
Passengers	193142	220000	225156	238748

All the above are for the calendar year except as noted-

(1) 12 months to 30 September
(2) 12 months to 30 September
(3) 9 months to 30 June
(4) 15 months to 30 September
(5) 12 months to 30 September
(6) 6 months to 31 March (these figures include totals for CAT operations).

Appendix 9   Histories of aircraft used by Silver City Airways

Bristol Freighter Mk 31 short nosed variants

Registration/ Construction no	Name	Variant	Allocation	From	To
G-AGVB 12731	none	2B	Bristol Aero Co	5/11/45	28/7/49
			F/F 30/4/46, del to Channel Island Airways 9/6/46, reg to Bowmaker Ltd but used by Silver City (through BAS) from Nov '48 <u>after</u> conv to Mk 21		
		21	Bowmaker Ltd	29/7/49	3/4/54
		21	SCA	15/4/54	6/2/57
			used on Berlin Airlift and for trooping as XF656 in 1955/56		
		21	to CAT as F-BHVB 2/57, w/o Feb 59 after hitting a beacon on ldg at Le Touquet.		
G-AGVC 12732		1	Bristol Aero Co	5/11/45	31/12/52
			F/F 23/6/46, del to SCA 2/7/48 after sales tour and Berlin Airlift and conv to Mk 31 prototype, wore Class B serial of G-18-2 for 1949 SBAC show, reconv to Mk 21 at end-51, del to SCA 12/2/52		
	City of Sheffield	21	SCA	19/6/53	28/11/61
			used for trooping as XF657 in 1955/56		
		21	Manx Airlines 1/12/61		
			u/c coll on ldg at Ronaldsway, IoM 30/6/62 and w/o 4/8/62.		
G-AHJC 12735		2A	Bristol Aero Co	30/5/46	23/6/49
			del to British American Air Services 7/46, used by SCA in India 1947, conv to Mk 21 for Berlin Airlift		
		21	to ANA as VH-INK 8/9/49, rtp 1961.		
G-AHJG 12739		2	Bristol Aero Co	24/7/46	19/4/47
			del to BAAS 14/9/46, conv to Mk 2A		
	Golden City	2A	del to Suidair as ZS-BOM 25/4/47		
		2A	Bristol Aero Co	16/9/47	28/8/48
		2A	del to SCA 18/10/47, used in India		
		21	del to Shell (Ecuador) as HC-SBU 27/8/48 cr in mountains at Salasaca 6/8/49.		
G-AHJI 12741		2A	Bristol Aero Co	24/7/46	30/11/46
		2A	del to Dalma Jain as VT-CHK 15/10/46		
		2A	Bristol Aero Co	6/1/50	25/4/50
			conv to Mk 21 April '50		
		21E	del to Aviacion y Co as EC-AES 4/5/50		
		21E	del to Air Outremer as F-DABI 17/12/50		
		21E	Air Kruise	2/12/55	28/10/57
	City of Bath	21E	SCA	28/10/57	31/12/62
		21E	to BAF	1/1/63	6/12/65 pwfu
G-AHJO 12747		2A	Bristol Aero Co	8/8/46	1/5/47
		2A	Bowmaker Ltd	5/5/47	28/7/49
			del to Skytravel 6/5/47, used by SCA on Berlin Airlift		
		2A	Bristol Aero Co	2/8/49	4/8/49 (conv)
		21M	del to Pakistan as G-781 (RPAF) 25/11/49.		
G-AHJP 12748		21E	Bristol Aero Co	8/8/46	21/4/48
		21E	to CAT as F-BENH		
		21E	SCA	28/3/51	28/11/53

Registration/ Construction no	Name	Variant	ARB registration dates Allocation	From	To
G-AHJP (contd)		21E	to Air Outremer as F-DABJ Jan 54		
		21E	to CGAN as F-OAUJ.		
G-AICM 12756		1	Bristol Aero Co del to Hunting Aerosurveys 12/12/47, conv to Mk 21	26/8/46	3/2/53
		21	SCA force-landed on railway lines near Berlin after diversions due to fog during Airlift on 19/1/53 and w/o.	April '51	4/3/53 pwfu.
G-AICS 12762		1	Bristol Aero Co	6/10/46	n/k
		1	del to Shell (Ecuador) as HC-SBN 1/4/47		
		21	Airwork	11/1/49	18/2/49
		21	Shell (London)	23/3/49	9/11/49
		21	del to Shell (Ecuador) as HC-SBZ 14/10/49		
		21	Aviation Traders	28/8/50	1/9/50
		21	BEA (used by Lancashire Aircraft Corporation)	7/9/50	3/4/57
		21	SCA on lease to Manx Airlines when it cr on Winter Hill nr Bolton 27/2/58 and w/o.	15/5/57	18/11/58 pwfu
G-AIFM 12773		21	Bristol Aero Co	11/10/46	14/5/48
		21	del to CAT as F-BEND 20/5/48		
		21	SCA op as Libyan Airways	3/12/51	1/3/54
		21	del to Air Outremer as F-DABK Jan 54		
		21	Air Kruise	7/1/56	28/10/57
	City of Carlisle	21	SCA	28/10/57	10/2/65 pwfu.
G-AIFV 12781		2A	Bristol Aero Co	11/10/46	27/10/47
		2A	del to Dalma Jain as VT-CID 4/12/46		
		21	Bristol Aero Co 2/5/49 for conv		
		21	SCA	28/3/50	31/12/52
	City of Manchester	21	(Libyan A/W)	31/12/52	17/6/54
		21	SCA dam at Wolverhampton airport during s/e overshoot May 1956, broken up 1962.	17/6/54	1/5/62 pwfu
G-AIME 12795		2A	Bristol Aero Co	3/12/46	14/8/47
		2A	del to Suidair as ZS-BVI 18/8/47 Bristol test a/c as R38 in late-'47		
		2A	Bristol Aero Co	23/1/48	14/11/50
		21	del to SCA	16/7/48	
		21	SCA used on Berlin Airlift and for trooping as XF662 in 1953	21/11/50	9/2/56
		21	Air Kruise	9/2/56	28/10/57
	City of Exeter	21	SCA	28/10/57	31/12/62
		21	BAF	1/1/63	2/6/64 pwfu.
G-AIMH 12798		21	Ministry of Aviation	3/12/46	7/12/48
		21	del to CAT as F-BECT 10/12/48		
	City of Birmingham	21	SCA used for trooping as XF663 in 1953/54	1/4/52	6/11/61
		21	Manx Airlines	9/11/61	31/12/62 pwfu
(G-AMLK - not taken up) 13073			Bristol Aero Co	23/8/51	31/3/53
G-AMWA			del SCA 31/3/53 in all-passenger layout and designated 'Super Wayfarer'		

Registration/ Construction no	Name	ARB registration dates Allocation	From	To
G-AMWA (contd)		United Dominions Trust (Commercial) Ltd	31/7/53	17/5/54
	City of London	SCA	19/5/54	3/4/62
		Britavia Ltd	3/4/62	1/1/63
		BUAF	1/1/63	24/9/63
		cr outside airport after engine failed on t/o from Guernsey in rain 24/9/63 and w/o.		
(G-AMPE - ntu) 13127		Bristol Aero Co	21/2/52	2/4/53
G-AMWB		SCA	2/4/53	13/1/56
		Bristol Aero Co	13/1/56	15/3/56
	City of Salisbury	SCA	9/4/56	3/4/62
		Britavia Ltd	3/4/62	21/3/68
		BUAF	1/1/63	1967 pwfu.
(G-AMPF - ntu) 13128		Bristol Aero Co	21/2/52	9/5/53
G-AMWC		SCA	9/5/53	1/1/56
		Bristol Aero Co	13/3/56	30/8/57
	City of Durham	SCA	30/8/57	3/4/62
		Britavia Ltd	3/4/62	17/4/67
		BUAF	1/1/63	17/4/67 pwfu.
(G-AMPG - ntu) 13131		Bristol Aero Co	21/2/52	29/5/53
G-AMWD		del SCA	29/5/53	1/1/56
		Bristol Aero Co	13/3/56	30/8/57
	City of Leicester	SCA	30/8/57	24/4/61
		to CAT as F-BKBD 26/4/61		31/12/62
G-AMWD		BUAF	1/1/63	17/4/67
		Britavia	7/1/63	17/4/67 pwfu.
(G-AMPH - ntu) 13132		Bristol Aero Co	21/2/52	11/6/53
G-AMWE		del to SCA	11/6/53	3/3/56
		Bristol Aero Co	3/3/56	30/8/57
	City of York	SCA	30/8/57	3/4/62
		BUAF	1/1/63	1966 pwfu
		Britavia Ltd	3/4/62	29/3/67 rtp.
(G-AMPI - ntu) 13133		Bristol Aero Co	21/2/52	23/6/53
G-AMWF		del SCA	23/6/53	3/3/56
		Bristol Aero Co	3/3/56	30/8/57
	City of Edinburgh	SCA	30/8/57	3/4/62
		Britavia	3/4/62	31/12/62
		BUAF	1/1/63	30/9/67
		BAF	30/9/67	21/3/68 rtp.
(G-ANMG - ntu) 13211		Bristol Aero Co	12/1/54	23/6/54
G-ANWG	City of Winchester	SCA	23/6/54	3/5/61
	Quatorze Juillet	to CAT as F-BKBG 5/61		1968 rtp.
(G-ANMH - ntu) 13212		Bristol Aero Co	12/1/54	6/7/54
G-ANWH	City of Hereford	SCA	6/7/54	3/4/62
		Britavia	3/4/62	7/1/63
	Onze Novembre	to CAT as F-BLHH 7/1/63		
		hit by a mechanical digger at Le Touquet and w/o 11/6/69.		

Registration/ Construction no	Name	ARB registration dates Allocation	From	To
(G-ANMI - ntu) 13213		Bristol Aero Co	12/1/54	23/7/54
G-ANWI	City of Glasgow Dix Huit Juin	SCA to CAT as F-BKBI	23/7/54 31/5/61	31/5/61 1968 rtp.
G-ANWJ 13254		Bristol Aero Co del SCA 1/6/56	31/1/56	1/6/56
	City of Bristol	SCA	28/9/56	3/4/62
		Britavia	3/4/62	5/2/71
		BUAF	1/1/63	30/9/67
		BAF	30/9/67	3/3/68 pwfu.
G-ANWK 13259		Bristol Aero Co del SCA	31/1/56 19/6/56	1/6/56
	The fourteenth of July/ la Quatorze Juillet	SCA	5/7/56	3/4/62
		Britavia Ltd	3/4/62	5/2/71
	City of Leicester	BUAF	1/1/63	30/9/67
		BAF	30/9/67	20/10/69 pwfu.
G-ANWL 13260	City of Worcester	Bristol Aero Co SCA cr at Guernsey 1/11/61 and pwfu.	31/1/56 20/7/56	11/7/56 29/12/61
G-ANWM 13261	City of Aberdeen	Bristol Aero Co SCA	31/1/56 10/7/56	1/4/57 3/4/62
		Britavia	3/4/62	22/1/68
		BUAF	1/1/63	22/1/68
		to CAT as F-BPIM	22/1/68	29/11/69
		BAF wfu October 1970, pwfu 5/2/71.	29/11/69	5/2/71
G-ANWN 13262		Bristol Aero Co del SCA 26/7/56	31/1/56	1/4/57
	City of Hull	SCA	30/4/57	3/4/62
		Britavia Ltd	3/4/62	2/1/68
		BUAF	1/1/63	30/9/67
		BAF	30/9/67	2/1/68
		to CAT as F-BPIN wfu 4/4/69, pwfu 5/2/71.	2/1/68	5/2/71

Other aircraft (from associated companies) used by Silver City Airways 1946-54

Registration Name		Construction no	Allocation	From	To
Airspeed Consul AS 65					
G-AIBF	none	3422	BAS	30/7/46	14/4/49
			SCA	2/5/49	19/3/54 pwfu.
G-AIKZ	none	4325	Airspeed Ltd	26/9/46	21/10/46
			Skytravel Ltd	29/10/46	8/1/48
			Bowmaker Ltd	21/1/48	12/3/51
			Lancashire A/c	20/4/51	2/4/55.
Avro 691 Lancastrian					
G-AHBT		1288	Min of Supply	20/2/46	17/8/46
	City of New York		BAS	17/8/46	6/6/47
	Sky Ranger		Skyways	9/7/47	24/3/52 rtp.
G-AHBV		1290	Min of Supply	20/2/46	10/10/46
	City of Canberra		BAS	10/10/46	25/9/47
			SCA	26/9/47	6/5/48
			A&IRC Ltd	17/6/48	14/3/49
			Skyways	16/3/49	7/3/52 rtp.

Registration	Name	Construction no	Allocation	From	To
G-AHBW		1291	Min of Supply	20/2/46	10/10/46
	City of London		BAS	10/10/46	21/1/48.

Breguet 761S

F-BASL (series 763 prototype - leased)			Breguet	June '53	September '53

de Havilland 90 Dragonfly

G-AEWZ (director's transport)			SCA	del '50	July '60

de Havilland 104 Dove 1B

G-AIWF		04023	BAS	20/11/46	25/11/47
			SCA	21/1/48	17/1/51
(ZS-DFA)			Commercial Air Services		
G-AIWF			Cambrian Airways (pre Services)		
				3/6/53	4/6/57
			Airviews Ltd	11/6/57	3/6/59
			Hants and Sussex Aviation Ltd		
				23/6/59	5/2/60
			Dan-Air Services Ltd		
				11/2/60	25/10/63
			Keegan Aviation Ltd		
				19/11/63	19/5/64.
G-AKJG		04071	SCA	23/10/47	10/3/51.
G-AKJP		04064	Amalgamated Tobacco Corp Ltd		
				21/10/47	June '48
			SCA	4/12/48	17/1/51
			Iraq Petroleum Transport Co Ltd		
				29/1/51	1/5/73.

Douglas C47A/Dakota series 3

G-AJAU City of Hollywood		12433	SCA	9/1/47	28/10/47.
G-AJAV		12386	SCA	9/1/47	6/9/50.

Lockheed 18-H Lodestar (prototype)
(Converted from Lockheed 14 in 1939)

(VP-TAE)			BWIA	1939	1947
G-AJAW		1954	BAS	18/1/47	25/11/47
			SCA	20/1/48	29/8/51.

Vickers-Supermarine Sea Otter

G-AJFU (ex JM747)			BAS	3/2/47	30/6/49
G-AJFV (ex JM959)			BAS	3/2/47	1/12/48
G-AJFW (ex JM957)			BAS	3/2/47	8/7/49.

Appendix 10   Histories of aircraft used by Air Charter Ltd

Registration/ Construction no	Name	Variant	ARB registration dates Allocation	From	To
Bristol Freighter 1950-65					
G-AHJI 12741		21E	see Appendix 9		
G-AICS 12762		21	see Appendix 9		
G-AIME 12795		21	see Appendix 9		
G-AMLP 13078	Vanguard	31E	Bristol Aero Co	23/8/51	9/2/53
		31E	Bristol Aero Co	17/2/53	4/11/53
			del to ACL	21/2/53	
		31E	ACL	4/11/53	–
			used on CAB ops from 2/9/54		
		32	ACL	4/7/58	31/3/65

Registration/ Construction no	Name	Variant	ARB registration dates Allocation	From	To	
G-AMLP (contd)		32	del BUAF	1/1/63		
		32	BUAF	13/4/65	30/9/67	
		32	BAF	30/9/67	13/11/70	
		32	Midland Air Cargo	16/11/70	11/6/71	
			to Canada as CF-QWJ 12/4/71.			
G-AMSA	Voyager	31E	Bristol Aero Co	1/4/52	31/8/55	
13142			del ACL	3/2/54		
			used on CAB ops from 2/9/54			
		31E	used for trooping in 1954/55 as XH385			
		31E	ACL	25/4/56	–	
			conv by ATEL	27/6/58		
		32	ACL	27/6/58	31/3/65	
			del BUAF	1/1/63		
		32	BUAF	13/4/65	17/4/67 pwfu.	
G-AMWA		32	see Appendix 9			
13073						
G-AMWB		32	see Appendix 9			
13127						
G-AMWC		32	see Appendix 9			
13128						
G-AMWD		32	see Appendix 9			
13131						
G-AMWE		32	see Appendix 9			
13132						
G-AMWF		32	see Appendix 9			
13133						
G-ANMF	Victory	31	Bristol Aero Co	12/1/54	31/8/55	
13216		31	ex G-18-192			
			del ACL/CAB	13/8/54		
		31	ACL	25/4/56	31/3/65	
			del BUAF	1/1/63		
		31	BUAF	13/4/65	30/9/67	
			wfu		31/8/67	
		31	BAF	30/9/67	26/8/70	rtp.
G-ANVR	Valiant	32	Bristol Aero Co	23/10/54	1/1/56	
13251			del ACL/CAB	25/3/55		
		32	Bristol Aero Co	3/3/56	1/12/57	
		32	ACL	24/12/57	31/3/65	
			del BUAF	1/1/63		
		32	BUAF	13/4/65	30/9/67	
		32	BAF	30/9/67	2/3/71	
			wfu	Oct 70	26/8/70	rtp.
G-ANVS	Vigilant	32	Bristol Aero Co	23/10/54	1/1/56	
13252			del ACL/CAB	5/4/55		
		32	Bristol Aero Co	3/3/56	1/12/57	
		32	Air Charter Ltd	24/12/57	31/3/65	
			del BUAF	1/1/63		
		32	BUAF	13/4/65	30/9/67	
		32	BAF	30/9/67	26/8/70	
			wfu	28/11/67	26/8/70	rtp.
G-ANWG		32	see Appendix 9			
13211						
G-ANWH		32	see Appendix 9			
13212						

Registration/ Construction no	Name	Variant	ARB registration dates Allocation	From	To
G-ANWI 13213		32	see Appendix 9		
G-ANWJ 13254		32	see Appendix 9		
G-ANWK 13259		32	see Appendix 9		
G-ANWM 13261		32	see Appendix 9		
G-ANWN 13262		32	see Appendix 9		
G-AOUU 13257	Venture	32	Bristol Aero Co del ACL/CAB	24/8/56 12/12/56	15/12/57
		32	Air Charter Ltd del BUAF	5/12/58 1/1/63	31/3/65
		32	BUAF	13/4/65	12/6/67 pwfu.
G-AOUV 13258	Valour	32	Bristol Aero Co del ACL/CAB	24/8/56 27/12/56	15/12/57
		32	Air Charter Ltd del BUAF	5/12/58 1/1/63	31/3/65
		32	BUAF on loan to Sabena from June 67	13/4/65	30/9/67
		32	BAF scrapped 1967	30/9/67	21/3/68 21/3/68 pwfu.
G-APAU 13256	Versatile	32 32	Bristol Aero Co ex G-18-203 del ACL/CAB	9/4/57 6/6/57	1/7/61
		32	Air Charter Ltd del BUAF	26/7/61 1/1/63	31/3/65
	City of Edinburgh	32 32 32 32	BUAF BAF Midland Air Cargo R J T Height	13/4/65 30/9/67 14/4/71 27/9/71	30/9/67 2/3/71 25/9/71 1974.
G-APAV 13263	Viceroy	32 32	Bristol Aero Co ex G-18-210 del ACL/CAB	9/4/57 18/4/57	1/7/61
		32	Air Charter Ltd del BUAF	26/7/61 1/1/63	31/3/65
		32 32 32 32 32	BUAF BAF Midland Air Cargo Capt C J O Trimble Shackleton Aviation 23/8/73.	13/4/65 30/9/67 18/11/70 13/6/72	30/9/67 6/11/70 10/5/72 23/8/73
G-ARSA 13169		31M 31M	del to RPAF as S4409 30/5/54 BUA b/u for spares at Southend.	5/7/61	22/6/64
EC-AAI 13126		31E	No details known		
EC-AHH 13125		31E	No details known		
EC-AHN 13075		31	No details known		

Registration/ Construction no	Name	Variant	ARB registration dates Allocation	From	To
Avro Tudor Type 688 variant					
G-AGRG		1	Min of A/c Prod	5/9/45	16/6/48
1255	Star Cressida		MCA	16/6/48	2/9/53
			Aviation Traders	14/9/53	27/7/54
			Air Charter	20/8/54	10/3/59
			conv to Super Trader 4 in 1956		
			cr 10/3/59 and w/o.		
G-AGRH		1	Min of A/c Prod	5/9/45	16/6/48
1256	Star Ceres		MCA	16/6/48	2/9/53
			Aviation Traders	14/9/53	27/7/54
			Air Charter	20/8/54	11/11/59 pwfu
			conv to Super Trader 4B in 1956.		
G-AGRI		1	Min of A/c Prod	5/9/45	16/2/50
1257	Star Oberon		MCA	16/2/50	2/9/53
			Aviation Traders	14/6/53	27/7/54
XF739			as Tudor 1 freighter, used for trooping flights in 1954 and serialled XF739		
G-AGRI			Air Charter	20/8/54	11/12/58 pwfu
G-AGRJ		1	Min of A/C Prod	5/9/45	16/6/48
1258	Star Celia		MCA	16/6/48	2/9/53
			Aviation Traders	14/9/53	27/7/54
	El Alamein		Air Charter	20/8/54	11/12/58
			as Tudor 1 freighter, withdrawn 1956 and pwfu 11/12/58.		
G-AHNI		1	Min of Supply	20/5/46	10/12/48
1342			BSAAC	21/12/48	3/9/49
			conv to Tudor 4B freighter circa 1948		
			BOAC (ntu)	3/9/49	21/10/49
	Star Olivia		MCA	21/10/49	2/9/53
			Aviation Traders	18/11/53	27/7/54
	Trade Winds		Air Charter	20/8/54	24/1/63 pwfu
			conv to prototype Super Trader 4B 1955.		
G-AHNL		1	Min of Supply	20/5/46	10/12/48
1345			conv to Tudor 4B freighter circa 1948		
			MCA	16/2/50	2/9/53
			Aviation Traders	18/11/53	27/7/54
			Air Charter	20/8/54	24/1/63 pwfu
			conv to Super Trader 4B 12/7/56.		
G-AHNM		1	Min of Supply	20/5/46	10/12/48
1346			conv to Tudor 4B freighter circa 1948		
	Star Cluster		MCA	16/2/50	2/9/53
			Aviation Traders	18/11/53	27/7/54
	Cirrus		Air Charter	20/8/54	24/1/63 pwfu
			conv to Super Trader 4B 13/2/58.		
G-AHNO		1	Min of Supply	20/5/46	10/12/48
1348			conv to Tudor 4B freighter circa 1948		
	Star Titania		MCA	16/2/50	2/9/53
			Aviation Traders	8/11/53	27/7/54
	Conqueror		Air Charter	20/8/54	24/1/63 pwfu
			conv to Super Trader 4B 12/7/56.		
G-AIYA		3	MCA	30/11/46	2/9/53
1367			carried Ministry prototype serial VP301		
			Aviation Traders	14/9/53	27/7/54
			conv to Tudor 1 circa 1954		
			Air Charter	28/8/54	13/11/58 pwfu.

Registration/ Construction no	Name	Variant	ARB registration dates Allocation	From	To
G-AJKC 1368		3	MCA	6/3/47	2/9/53
			carried Ministry prototype serial VP312		
			Aviation Traders	14/9/53	27/7/54
			Air Charter	20/8/54	1/12/58 pwfu
			withdrawn 1956 and pwfu 1/12/58.		

Avro Tudor Type 689 variant

Registration/ Construction no	Name	Variant	ARB registration dates Allocation	From	To
G-AGRX/1261 VX199		7	Min of Supply	24/9/45	30/10/53
			temporarily serialled TS883 until VX199		
			carried between 8/1/51 and Oct 53		
G-AGRX			Flight Refuelling	30/10/53	4/1/54
			Aviation Traders	3/3/54	3/4/59 pwfu
			withdrawn for spares 1955.		
G-AGRY/1262		2	Min of Supply	24/9/45	1/9/48
			Airflight Ltd	1/9/48	2/12/48
			DCT Bennett	6/12/48	26/1/49
			Airflight Ltd	17/3/49	13/7/49
			DCT Bennett	15/7/49	20/3/50
			Fairflight Ltd	28/4/50	12/6/59
VX202			Min of Supply ops		1953
XF537			serial for trooping flights		1953
			withdrawn from use 1958.		
G-AGRZ/1263 VZ366		2	Min of Supply	30/9/45	30/10/53
			VZ366 carried between 8/1/51 and Oct 53		
			Flight Refuelling	30/10/53	4/1/54
			Aviation Traders	3/3/54	3/4/59 pwfu
			withdrawn from use 1956.		
G-AKBY/1417		2	MCA	16/8/47	25/9/48
			conv to Mk 5 25/9/48		
		5	Airflight Ltd	25/9/48	2/12/48
			DCT Bennett	6/12/48	26/1/49
			Airflight Ltd	17/3/49	13/7/49
			DCT Bennett	15/7/49	12/3/50
			cr at Sigingstone, Glamorgan 12/3/50 and w/o.		
G-AKBZ/1418		2	MCA	16/8/47	4/11/48
			conv to Mk 5 circa 1948		
		5	BSAAC	19/11/48	3/9/49
	Star Falcon		BOAC	3/9/49	1/11/51
			purchased for US operator 11/51 but ntu in open store until wfu in 1956.		
G-AKCA/1419		2	MCA	16/8/47	8/12/48
			conv to Mk 5 circa 1948		
		5	BSAAC	9/12/48	3/9/49
	Star Hawk		BOAC	3/9/49	21/9/51
			SFS	5/10/51	23/5/52
			purchased for US operator 11/51 but ntu to Canada as CF-FCY.		
G-AKCB/1420		2	MCA	10/8/47	8/12/48
			conv to Mk 5 circa 1948		
		5	BSAAC	29/12/48	3/9/49
	Star Kestrel		BOAC	3/9/49	1/11/51
			purchased for US operator 11/51 but ntu withdrawn from use 1955.		

Appendix 10 (Continued)

Registration/ Construction no	Name	Variant	ARB registration Allocation	dates From	To
G-AKCD/1422		2	MCA	16/8/47	7/2/49
			conv to Mk 5 circa 1948		
		5	BSAAC	8/2/49	3/9/49
	Star Eagle		BOAC	3/9/49	1/9/50
			William Dempster Ltd	9/9/50	1/3/54
			Air Charter	5/4/54	29/1/59 pwfu

Abbreviations used in appendices

F/F	first flight	del	delivered	reg	registered
conv	conversion	w/o	written off	ldg	landing
u/c	undercarriage	coll	collapsed	rtp	reduced to produce
cr	crashed	pwfu	permanently withdrawn from use		
dam	damaged	op	operated	s/e	single-engined
a/c	aircraft	t/o	takeoff	ntu	not taken up
wfu	withdrawn from use	ops	operations	b/u	broken up

ARB   Air Registration Board   SCA   Silver City Airways
BAS   British Aviation Services   CAT   Compeigne Air Transport
BAAS   British American Air Services   ANA   Australian National Airlines
BAF   British Air Ferries   BEA   British European Airways
BUAF   British United Air Ferries   BWIA   British West Indies Airlines
A&IRC Ltd   Aeronautical & Industrial Research Corporation Ltd
ACL   Air Charter Ltd   CAB   Channel Air Bridge
RPAF   Royal Pakistan Air Force   BUA   British United Airways
BSAAC   British South American Airlines Corporation   SFS   Surrey Flying Services
MCA   Ministry of Civil Aviation   BOAC British Overseas Airways Corporation

Freighter Mk 32 F-BLHH 'Dix Huit Juin' of British United's associated French company Compeigne Air Transport at Lydd in August 1966. CAT Freighters had their individual names interchanged frequently. Three years later, and still operated by CAT, it was hit by a mechanical digger at Le Touquet and written off (photo by Paul Doyle).

Bibliography

The Aeroplane magazine 13 June 1947 & 4 July 1952

The Aeroplane and *Commercial Aviation News* magazine, January 1965

Aer Turas - a short history (R J Killen) Aviation News 15 March 1974

Air Bridge 2 - the design, development and service use of the ATL98 *Carvair* conversions and their effect on the civilian vehicle air ferry era (Paul A Doyle) Pub: Forward Airfield Research Publishing 2000

Air Ferry - The story of Silver City and Channel Air Bridge (Douglas Whybrow) Pub: by Tourism International 1995

Airfield Review magazine (various issues) Pub: Airfield Research Group (quarterly)

Airways magazine, February 2001

Aviation Traders Engineering Ltd company archives

Bristol Aircraft (J D Oughton) Pub: Ian Allan

The Bristol Freighter (feature articles) *Aeroplane* magazine July 2002

The Bristol 170 (J D Oughton) Aircraft Illustrated, Feb-May 1969

British Civil Aircraft from 1916 (A J Jackson) Pub: Putnam

The Channel Air Bridge press library

The Channel Hop (E S Turner) Punch magazine 2 April 1958

Citroën magazine July 1980

Richard Costain Ltd house magazines nos 133, 153 & 157

The Devil Casts His Net - The Winter Hill Air Disaster (Steve Morrin) Pub: Author 2005

Flight magazine (various)

The flight log books of Captains D B Cartlidge, A English and P E Rosser

Fly Me, I'm Freddie! (R Eglin & B Ritchie) Pub: Weidenfeld and Nicholson 1980

Golden Age - Commercial Aviation in Britain 1945-66 (Charles Woodley) Pub: Airlife 1993

A History of Aviation in Essex (edited by K Cole) Pub: RAeS (Southend branch) 1967

Lydd Airport visitors book

Ministry of Transport and Civil Aviation airfield landing charts (War Office publications)

The Rise and Fall of the Air Ferries (James Montgomerie) Aviation News Vol 22 No 8

Peaceful Fields (John F Hamlin) Pub: GMS Enterprises 1996

Pooleys flight guides

Silver City Airways press library.

Authors pages

The author, a member of the Airfield Research Group and the Mosquito Aircraft Museum, is a structural engineer currently living in Hertfordshire and has worked extensively with the Defence Estates Organisation on behalf of the United States 3rd Air Force in the UK before moving back into the public sector.

After flying with the United States 3rd Air Force Aero Club organisation around the UK from RAF Lakenheath and Mildenhall, he has also operated American aircraft types out of Norwich and Elstree as well as a WW1 RAF airfield in Bedfordshire. He and his wife currently fly vintage de Havilland aircraft types from Cambridgeshire.

After completing his previous work on the vehicle air ferry which used the Aviation Traders *Carvair* from 1962 to 1977, this book is the 'prequel' in this saga of British ingenuity in aviation and, although much has already been written about the subject either in magazine articles or books, the author considers that it is the most in-depth survey of the formulative and ongoing years of the vehicle air ferry.

Still available from Forward Airfield Research Publishing:

AIR BRIDGE 2

*The design, development and service use of the ATL98 Carvair
conversions and their effect on the civilian vehicle air ferry era*

The Carvair was a British innovation designed for the carriage of vehicles and freight as a replacement for the Bristol Freighter. This book details the concept, design, wind tunnel tests carried out, constructional details and flight test data. In-service use of the type with various airlines from 1962-77 is recorded along with all notable incidents, plus a concise history of each of the 21 aircraft converted, as well as diagrams and appendices.

The book, to A4 format in softback with laminated cover, contains 112 pages and 48 black & white photographs, many not previously published.

£14.50 (by post in UK) use ISBN 0 9525624 7 2 when ordering from booksellers

also still available –

'Where the Lysanders were...'
(the story of Sawbridgeworth's airfields)

A comprehensive history of flying at this Hertfordshire location from 1912 to the present day, listing operational units, aircraft and building types. From a First World War emergency landing ground, through the mid-war flying circus years, and on into the Second World War as an important Army Co-Operation airfield, with Lysander, Mosquito, Mustang and Spitfire aircraft just some of the types operated from the site, this book gives all you ever wanted to find out about a site previously missed by researchers.

Plans show development of the flying sites, layout and details of all buildings. Appendices detail Commanding Officers, resident aircraft types, aircraft serials and their units, and a full listing is given of all aerial incidents at or near the airfield.

The book, to A4 format in softback with laminated cover, contains 96 pages with 40 black and white photographs, plus many maps, diagrams and appendices.

£13.00 (by post in UK) use ISBN 0 9525624 0 5 when ordering from booksellers

also now available –

Aviation Memorials of Essex

*A gazetteer of the memorials to feats of aviation in the County,
and the story behind each one*

This book locates each memorial, no matter where or in what form it is, connected with feats of aviation in Essex over the period before, during and after both World Wars. It gives the reason for each memorial, the history attached to it, and how it was instigated.

The book, to A4 format in softback with laminated cover, contains 84 pages with 75 black & white photographs, maps and appendices.

£14.00 (by post in UK) use ISBN 0 9525624 9 9 when ordering from booksellers.

Still available from Forward Airfield Research Publishing:

Fields of the First

A history of aircraft landing grounds in Essex used during the First World War

by Paul A Doyle

When the First World War started the County had no service aerodromes, aircraft being flown into Essex from training stations well to the west of London as and when required for operational needs, but by the end of that conflict a total of 31 landing grounds had been laid down over different periods of time for use by all 3 services.

From the major sites known as Flight Stations and where squadrons were based, aircraft flew patrols around the clock but, as no form of early warning system existed at that time, they had to fly set patrol lines which could not be deviated from unless actually in an attack on the enemy. If lost, damaged or caught out by bad weather, or pilots were unable to reach their home station, they had emergency landing grounds provided across the County. Thus many of the smaller sites, generally grass fields with basic lighting aids, came into being.

Covering the County of Essex as it was in 1918 the book includes landing grounds that are now within the Greater London area. The history of each is given, plus the notable events that occurred there, and the tenure by the service units allocated to the site. Many of them were used, or planned to be used, for other aviation or military purposes and accordingly their subsequent history is given. A site plan, showing buildings constructed during the First World War, is supported by a current aerial photo to depict the location as it is now.

Two final chapters detail the buildings remaining from the period, and memorials raised across the County to feats of aviation in the First World War. Another section deals with the intrusions by German airships and what visible remains exist from them in the County, whilst the story of the struggles by British airmen to bring them down is also recorded.

Eight appendices detail the aerial combat patrol lines used, operational periods for the landing grounds in chart form, the ultimate organisation of the Home Defence squadron network, ground signals used on the landing grounds, building location plans for each of the Flight Stations, building drawings, the costs of aircraft and engines in the First World War, plus comprehensive listings of personnel and equipment numbers at the Flight Stations.

The book, to A4 format in softback with laminated cover, contains 120 pages, 50 black & white photographs (many aerial shots), plus landing ground maps, diagrams and appendices.

The work gained a high commendation in the 1997 Essex Book Awards scheme.

£15.00 (by post in UK) use ISBN 0 9525624 1 3 when ordering through booksellers